# RAISED BED GARDENING FOR BEGINNERS

## CREATE A HEALTHY, SUSTAINABLE GARDEN AND GROW YOUR OWN ORGANIC VEGETABLES IN JUST 3 DAYS WITH NO DIGGING

JULIE GARNER

# CONTENTS

## A FREE Special Gift to Our Readers

Included with your purchase of this book is a checklist of 83 Ways Anyone Can Become More Self-sufficient Anywhere In One Hour.

Visit the link RIGHT NOW or scan the QR code and claim your FREE bonus gift!

**www.julie-garner.com**

# INTRODUCTION

If you're looking for dirt on what being outside can do for you, I'm happy to dig it up!

Most Americans spend a staggering 93% of their lives indoors. This is made up of 87% spent inside buildings and 6% inside vehicles, leaving only 7% to make up the amount of time that the average American spends outside (Kleipis et al., 2001). That is seriously unbalanced!

The benefits of being outside in nature have been shown to have tremendous effects on your physical and mental well-being. These benefits include but are not limited to a lowered risk of anxiety, and depression, improved short-term memory skills, and healthier blood pressure levels. Being outdoors will help make you feel more focused and present in the moment, which will result in enjoying life to its fullest (Fortier, 2019).

Many people are looking for ways to connect to the earth and their environments, and there is nothing better and more fulfilling than learning how to grow your own food!

## GROUNDING OR EARTHING

The earth has a natural electrical charge; thankfully, a negative one, or it would be a bit shocking for all of us! Jokes aside, with this electrical current coursing through the earth, all electrical systems installed need to be grounded, or what is also known as being "earthed." People can also benefit from practicing grounding themselves. The most straightforward way to do this is to walk barefoot outside or work in the garden with your hands. When allowing your bare skin to touch uncovered earth, it creates an energy flow from the ground into your body, resulting in health benefits. Getting our hands into the dirt and soaking up the sunshine on our skin as we pull weeds, till the soil, plant seeds, water them, and harvest, is nature's purest medicine.

### *Sharing My Passion*

Being fortunate to grow up on an old farm is enough to make anyone fall in love with the outdoors. This is where my passion for gardening had sprung—pun intended. My memories of being a young child involve the lush outdoor gardens that always surrounded our home. I would spend hours outdoors helping my aunt and my grandmother take care of their gardens from a young age. Learning to till the soil, pull weeds, plant seeds, and eventually harvest ripe fruits and vegetables was one of the most rewarding aspects of my childhood. The freshly bloomed raspberries and strawberries we gathered tasted all the better for the work that we put in. To this day, I use the knowledge passed down from my family members to maintain my garden and grow my own organic food at home.

And now, I'm passing that torch, along with this knowledge, on to you.

I wanted to share the benefits of growing food outdoors at home with anyone who might be curious about starting a garden of their own. At-home gardening doesn't just make you more self-sufficient; it also grants you more control over what you're putting into your body. Growing your own fruits and vegetables will bring you the most flavorful and nutritious meals you've ever eaten while *also* letting you avoid the synthetic chemicals and pesticides lingering on the produce in the grocery store. Furthermore, the rewarding feeling of watching seeds grow and bloom into food under your care is something that everyone deserves to experience.

Gardening using the raised beds method can be any shape, but we'll be using the example of rectangular wood beds in this book for the most part. It is my preferred method for excellent results. We'll be going over the benefits of using raised beds and the best materials and techniques for building your beds. Since the layout of your garden is a critical part of a successful garden, we'll also be talking about how to make sure each of your plants gets the correct amount of sunlight they require to flourish.

Alternatively, learning how to choose the best fruits, vegetables, and herbs to grow in a raised bed garden, the specifics of their care, which plants are best placed together, and which are best kept apart are all covered in this book. Finally, we'll look into protecting your garden from threats like pests and weeds and how to overcome the common challenges that all new and experienced gardeners face.

This book will help you set yourself up for success every season.

Raised bed gardening is an ancient practice that is growing in popularity today. If you're reading this book, congratulations! You've already taken your first steps toward bringing your food production into your own hands, finding a deeper connection to nature, and growing healthy and delicious produce right outside your back door.

# 1

# INTRODUCTION TO RAISED BED GARDENING

*The glory of gardening: hands in the dirt, head in the sun, heart with nature. To nurture a garden is to feed not just the body, but the soul.*

— ALFRED AUSTIN

While raised bed gardening is an ancient practice, it's become increasingly popular recently with a movement of people deciding to find ways to become more self-sufficient. Pinterest, Instagram, and other social media websites have jumped onto the craze. A cursory search will show you endless pictures of immaculate, photogenic gardens growing in everything from wooden frames to antique bathtubs! While your garden will start much smaller, you can plant raised bed gardens in various "beds" or containers.

Raised bed gardens can be used to grow flowers, vegetables, and anything that fits in the bed being used. It opens up a wide range of options for where and how you'll be setting up your garden and makes gardening accessible to people who wouldn't have been able to plant a traditional garden. In this chapter, we'll be going over the many benefits of raised bed gardening and how this practice is distinguished from regular gardening.

## BENEFITS OF RAISED BED GARDENING

### *Raised Beds Are Extremely Versatile*

One of the first and foremost benefits of raised bed gardening is that it is incredibly flexible and versatile. Raised beds can be constructed from various materials, including wood, stone, bricks, synthetic boards, food-grade plastic, and even hay bales. As long as it won't contaminate the food, you can build a raised bed out of practically anything, including the material you may already have lying around. You can also create a raised bed without a frame by piling up the soil until it's elevated. This means almost anyone can start raised bed gardening without breaking the bank. You just need to be ready to dig in and get your hands dirty—pun intended!

### *You Can Plant (Almost) Anywhere*

Anywhere is a bit of an overstatement, but not by much. Closely related to the last point, raised bed gardens make it possible to grow your own produce anywhere you have room to establish one (or many) as long as there is optimal sunlight!

Never mind if you have limited space or even no garden at all, this should not prevent you from pursuing this method of gardening. Perhaps you have just a balcony, a patio, or a tiny postage stamp garden; raised bed gardens can work just about anywhere. If the climate permits, and you have something to fill with soil that can be used to establish your raised bed, you are already halfway there. Even if your soil is of poor quality or perhaps contaminated, this should not halt you in your pursuit of growing your own food to eat.

There are vast swathes of land where the soil quality stops you from gardening straight into the ground to grow food to consume. For example, depending on the area, some regions can be very dry or wet and marshy, which does not permit traditional gardening. This is yet another reason raised bed gardening is a great option!

The one caveat is that raised bed gardening is practiced outdoors. While it's possible to grow food inside with the right equipment, that's an entirely different book than this one, as indoor gardening comes with its own unique set of rules and practices.

### You Pick the Soil

You are allowed much more choice when it comes to deciding what kind of soil you will be using. It's common sense that higher-quality fertile soil helps plants grow more quickly and easily, resulting in a much better harvest than one planted in lower-quality soil.

The soil in a raised bed also "tills" itself as roots make room for themselves as they grow. Many people dislike tilling in the first place since it can ruin the structure of the soil and cause it to lose nutrients. Therefore, the raised bed method allows you to layer your compost and other fertilizers on top of the soil without breaking a sweat! Worms can also help stir the soil in a raised bed garden as they wriggle around.

### It's Accessible

Many people who like to garden might have accessibility needs that prevent them from enjoying and experiencing this pastime. For example, people with a more limited range of motion or those who suffer from joint or back pain can benefit from raised beds as they require less bending over, crouching, and rising than planting straight into the ground.

The fantastic news is that your physical limitations do not prevent you from enjoying your garden, as raised beds can be modified and customized to any desired height. If it is easier for you to garden at waist height rather than on the ground, raised beds can be designed with these accessibility needs in mind.

### Raised Beds Keep Plants Safe.

Raised beds are set up perfectly to help plants grow and thrive while protecting them from pests and other threats at the same time.

Let's look at the bane of every gardener for a minute: weeds. While you can try your best to pull or kill weeds before they become a problem, there's little you can do to stop them from getting into your garden in the first place—or is there?

As you might have guessed, raised beds reduce how many weeds and other invasive plants like crabgrass you may have to contend with. Firstly, as you don't have to till the soil, you won't be inadvertently mixing unwanted seeds into your garden before you even start planting. You can also cover your raised beds to kill off any weeds growing before the planting season begins. A lack of sunlight will kill weeds every time, so blocking out the sun with newspaper, cardboard, a tarp, or even mulch will smother them in a pinch. While you may still get some weeds, their invasion will be at a much smaller scale than in a traditional garden and will be able to be removed with ease as your soil will be good quality, not hard and compact.

Since you can access "underneath" the soil of a raised bed garden, you can put in barriers like chicken wire or hardware cloth against burrowing critters to stop them from ruining your plants. If you use animal repellents, they don't have to go straight on the plants; you can apply them around the bed's perimeter instead, making it easier to keep harmful chemicals off your food. You can also easily modify your beds to include deer fencing, bird nets, or whatever else you feel you need to keep your plants safe to ensure the local wildlife doesn't eat your harvest before your family can!

Raised beds also allow for better drainage than regular gardens—that's just a fact of gravity! Most plants do better in well-drained soil, and water drains away from plants in a raised bed much more quickly than it would drain from the ground itself. This can also protect your plants from a heavy rainfall that would have been damaging to a traditional garden!

Finally, while this is more of a "bonus" that doesn't happen every time, raised beds are so good at protecting some plants that sometimes plants will unexpectedly survive over winter. It can be amazing to discover that plants you've worked hard to care for made it to the following spring, and caring for them once again in a new growing season can be very rewarding.

### Better Harvests (In More Ways Than One)

Raised beds put you in complete control over how your food is grown, which (if any) compounds or pesticides are used to treat the plants, and ultimately, what goes into your body when you finally get to eat the plants you've worked so hard to grow! Think about it: While you *think* the food in the grocery store contains a safe level of pesticides or chemical fertilizers, do you know that for sure? Do you want to risk it for your family?

Choosing a raised bed garden takes the risk completely out of the equation and allows *you* to decide which fertilizers and pest control methods you're comfortable using. Many people are skeptical of the benefits of organic produce, but it really makes a world of difference. Organic foods are healthier than their non-organic counterparts for many reasons. We've already touched on the fact that organic food from a raised bed garden will not contain chemical pesticides. However, even when not considering that, they still contain many more vitamins and minerals than the produce you'll find at the grocery store. Since the food doesn't have to be transported miles away by truck before it lands on your dinner table, it'll also be fresher when you consume it. Taking into account that nutrients degrade over time, this is another reason why the food in your raised bed will be better for you than the food in the grocery store.

 You will also get *more* produce from raised beds than from a traditional one, both by the number of plants and their weight. Having the opportunity to pick high-quality soil means you'll have higher yields, which means growing bigger, better, and more robust plants. Unlike traditional gardening, where rows or paths are created for walking, raised beds allow you to utilize all the space to grow *more*.

If your raised beds are on a balcony or patio, they can be raised high enough to create great storage space underneath for your gardening tools. The benefits are endless.

Now that we've explored the benefits of raised bed gardening, you might be eager to get started! In the next chapter, we'll be starting to explore the essential gardening tools you will need and how you can set up a garden of your own in just three days.

# 2

# DAY ONE—THE PLANNING PROCESS

*When the world wearies and society fails to satisfy, there is always the garden.*

— MINNIE AUMONIER

S ince raised bed gardening involves economizing space, your garden layout is critically important to get the most out of your plants. Even with a traditional garden, you can't just go outside, toss some seeds on the ground, and expect a beautiful harvest in a few weeks! Planning a successful garden takes just that: *planning*, and this isn't a step where you want to cut corners. Before you get started, you'll need to think about what you want your raised bed garden to look like and what tools and materials you will need to achieve your goal. This chapter will cover Day One of the three days it takes to set up a raised bed garden for beginners, which is the planning phase.

 As you read through this chapter, consider keeping a note-book, scrap paper, or your favorite device by your side, where you can start sketching out what *your* garden plan might look like. You may want to make lists of things to pick up or draw a diagram of where you will place your garden beds. This will come in handy tomorrow/in the next chapter, where we'll start putting your plan into motion.

## BASIC GARDENING TOOLS

My intention of applying the raised bed gardening method involves no digging–more on that later–but that doesn't mean you don't need the right tools to get the job done! Our intention in this section is not to have you go out and break the bank but to indicate which items will make your gardening journey more effortless, efficient, and fun. The right tools make working in your garden a pleasure instead of a chore, which I believe gardening should be. Consider this: You wouldn't use a butter knife to cut raw carrots, and you probably wouldn't cook carrots often if that were all you had to cut them with! Your hand would probably start to hurt from the effort you had to put in. It works the same way with gardening. Using dull, low-quality, or incorrect tools in your garden will increase your risk of injury and cause unnecessary strain on your body. It will also take the fun out of gardening by making each small task a source of frustration. Therefore, it's crucial to invest in the right tools before getting started.

While high-quality tools can be expensive, it's helpful to consider them an *investment*. They might cost a little more at first, but you'll be saving money in the long run, as high-quality tools won't break as quickly as their cheaper counterparts. Not only that, but since quality tools make it easier to create the garden you want, they'll pay for themselves over time, as you'll be spending less on groceries thanks to your delicious organic harvest! That old saying, "Penny wise, pound foolish," rings bells!

Without further ado, I've included a list below of the recommended tools for a beginner raised bed gardener, along with explanations of their functions and what you'll be using them for.

## *Gloves*

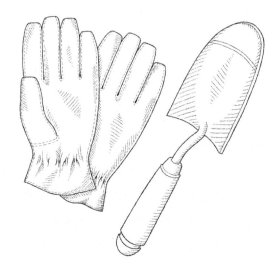

Before we get into the equipment you'll be adding to your garden shed or toolbox; we need to start with the proper personal protection equipment that any gardener needs: a sturdy pair of gardening gloves. Gardening gloves are made with various materials, including leather, canvas, and cotton, to neoprene and other synthetic materials. Regardless of what they're made of, gardening gloves protect your hands and wrists from injury when you're hard at work in your garden. They guard against splinters, thorns, brambles, and other plant parts that can injure your bare hands while improving your grip and preventing slippage when working with tools.

A decent pair of gloves is an essential part of any gardener's toolbox, but not all gloves are created equal, and a pair of gloves that work for one person may not work for another. When selecting your gardening gloves, there are certain things you need to look out for. A pair of gardening gloves should be thick enough to protect your hands and withstand wear and tear but thin enough that they don't interfere with your grip. Gloves that are too bulky can make it harder to do delicate tasks like uprooting and replanting seedlings. Secondly, you want your gloves to fit snug enough not to slip off at a dangerous moment, but they should not be so tight that they restrict your range of motion. Finally, you want gloves with cuffs long enough to protect your wrists from branches and thorns when working with your plants. It's best to try a few pairs on at the store, try to pick tools up, and see what you're most comfortable with before making a purchase. Gloves are an essential tool, but also try to take some time to do a little gardening without gloves when the conditions allow for it. As mentioned previously, using bare hands in the soil is a wonderful way to connect with the earth. The feeling of soil in your hands is quite incredible, too!

### Watering Tools

As you already know, watering your plants is a significant and necessary part of gardening. Different plants need varying amounts of water to grow properly, and therefore various tools have been invented to make delivering water much more manageable.

Garden hoses with adjustable nozzles are the most important watering tool in your garden toolbox. Your garden hose should be long enough to let you reach every corner of your garden comfortably, and it should come with a nozzle that enables you to control the water pressure coming out. Keep in mind that longer hoses have lower water pressure overall. Storing your hose out of the sun in a neat coil will make it last longer than storing it in a pile, as kinks in the hose can obstruct water flow in the short term and create cracks that will cause leaks over time.

Watering wands are attachments you add to the end of a garden hose to break up or distribute water flow. These allow you to evenly distribute water over a garden bed without drowning your plants. Since watering wands have long and straight handles, unlike a garden hose, you can also use your watering wand to get in hard-to-reach places. A wand that is too long will be just as inconvenient as one that is too short. Secondly, consider a watering wand with a shut-off valve on the handle, as this allows you to turn off or adjust the flow of water instantly. The environment, and your plants, will thank you!

The most classic watering tool in every garden shed is a watering can. These gently sprinkle water onto plants, with the added convenience that they can transport a relatively large amount of water at a time. Watering cans are made of plastic or metal. Plastic will be more lightweight in most cases but are less durable. A two-handled design might suit you better than the classic one-handle if you have physical limitations. It allows you to exert additional control and stability over the can.

### Turning the Soil

Our method for raised bed gardening does not involve digging; however, with any gardening, there are times when you will need to work with and move the soil itself! Depending on the task and how much dirt you need to move, you can use various tools.

You may need a gardening fork to break up the soil before planting or loosen the soil to remove large rocks. Gardening forks are spade-sized tools with tines or prongs at the ends that resemble a rake or pitchfork and come in a range of different styles with different purposes. Gardening forks are great for manipulating hardened or densely packed dirt. Gardening forks with curved tines can lift and move things, like when you want to add compost or mulch to the top of your garden bed. Straight tines are more helpful in loosening tightly packed soil. Choose a gardening fork with square rather than flat tines, as these are much stronger and can withstand more resistance without snapping off.

Hand trowels are used for various tasks: from digging out weeds to moving young plants between containers. These come in different shapes and sizes that are ideal for different tasks. A wide or broad blade can be used to create indentations in the soil, perfect for replanting a row of new seedlings. On the other hand, moving individual plants is better accomplished with a narrow, pointed trowel. Be careful in choosing a trowel that isn't too big for your hand, as a slipping hand trowel can give you a nasty cut if you're unlucky.

Hoes are similar to hand trowels in some ways but have a long handle that allows you to manipulate dirt and other materials on the ground without bending over. Like hand trowels, hoes come in different shapes, specialized for different uses. For example, a broad, flat hoe can be used for creating rows to plant vegetables in, while hula or stirrup hoes are better for cutting up and removing unwanted plants and weeds. Keep in mind a sharper hoe will be better at its task while minimizing collateral damage at the same time. This is especially important if you're trying to dig around perennial plants you want to preserve.

Rakes are a similar tool that every gardener should keep on hand if you need to clean up fallen leaves or other yard debris. Rakes can sometimes also spread mulch or compost on top of your garden. Opt for a plastic rake if you want them to be flexible with a gentler touch. If you want something solid and durable, go for a metal variety instead. It is helpful to have both.

Of course, we can't finish this section without talking about your classic spade! Even if you're not digging holes, it doesn't mean that one of these won't be helpful to have on hand. Your trusty spade has your back whenever you need a little extra leverage to move soil or compost or replant something too large for your hand trowel. Look for a spade with an ash hardwood handle and a stainless steel head if you want something that will last you for years without succumbing to wear and tear.

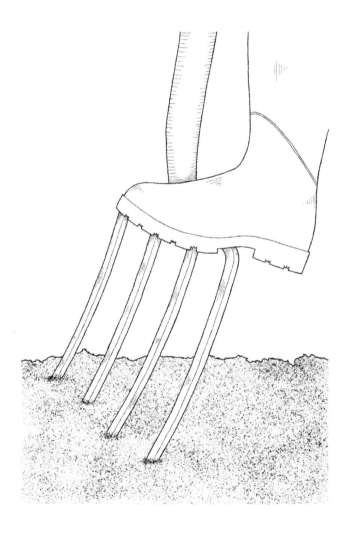

### *Shears and Loppers*

## ▷ Shears

As you know, gardening requires you to safely cut (or snip) pieces off plants at certain times. For safety reasons, it's crucial to have a sharp tool to use for this so that you don't cut yourself on a blunt slipping tool. Furthermore, using a sharp tool protects the plant by minimizing how much stress and damage is inflicted on the part you're *not* cutting off. Clean cuts are what a plant needs.

Garden hedge shears look like a giant pair of scissors and are used to prune trees and shrubs that are getting out of hand or otherwise encroaching on other plants' space.

The two shears most commonly sold in gardening stores are: anvil pruners and bypass pruners. Anvil pruners cut plants between a sharp blade and a flat surface. These are best for cutting dead wood or plants. This tool's "rougher" action allows you to cut through the dried and hardened stems of dead plants but can cause unnecessary damage to living plants that are more flexible.

On the other hand, bypass pruners are scissors. They use two sharp edges passing by each other to cut plants, making them a more precise way of cutting off live stems and leaves without damaging the rest of the plant.

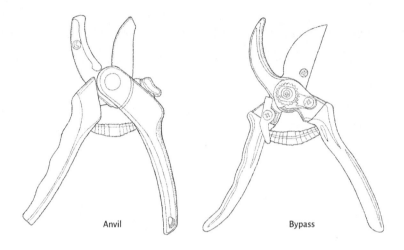

Anvil    Bypass

Ratcheting pruners are a sub-set of anvil pruners and have a particular hinge action that gives them extra strength without too much effort, which can be great if you have very woody, tough plants on your hands. These can also be helpful to people with limited physical strength or abilities. For example, if you have arthritis or otherwise struggle with repetitive physical work using your hands, you may want to choose a pair with ratcheting action.

When picking out a pair of pruners or shears, look for a pair that you can hold and use comfortably. Being able to control the tool in the palm of one hand is a good indicator that it's the right size. You don't want to be struggling with a sharp tool when you're trying to work with it.

## ▷ **Loppers**

Loppers, like shears, are scissor-like tools used for cutting plants. They are used to gain access to those hard-to-reach places that you can't get to with handheld pruners. Having longer handles makes them less precise, especially for more minor cuts, making them far more helpful for thicker branches due to the increased leverage.

Loppers, however, come with the drawback that they can get cumbersome, especially if they're on the longer side–some have handles up to 36 inches in length.

Therefore, before buying a pair of loppers, think about what you're going to be cutting and choose a pair that won't be too cumbersome. The material of the loppers also matters when it comes to weight; aluminum and copper handles are remarkably lightweight and easy to use.

Sharpening or having your tools sharpened regularly is one of the best things you can do for yourself to prevent an accident. Remember, loppers and shears are like knives in that sharper tools are always safer. Blunt instruments are more likely to slip, which can be very dangerous.

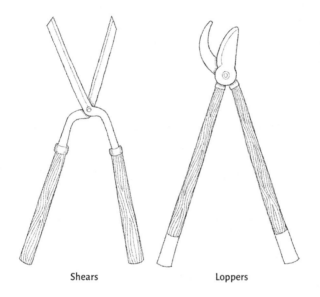

Shears                    Loppers

## Wheelbarrows

Wheelbarrows are great for protecting your back from strain when transporting dirt or compost from one place to another. Trying to do this with a shovel or spade is a recipe for injury and is also more time-consuming. Wheelbarrows can also quickly transport building materials or tools that otherwise require multiple trips. A trusty wheelbarrow is necessary to make your gardening tasks as streamlined as possible.

When shopping for a wheelbarrow, don't restrict yourself to the classic dual-handled and one-wheeled variety, as these can be easy to tip over in motion. Instead, consider a dual-wheeled and one-handled wheelbarrow. Unlike typical counterparts, these can be pushed or pulled, making them easier to move over uneven terrain. They're also steadier, making them easier to use if you have physical limitations. As with the rest of your garden tools, don't forget to take good care of your wheelbarrow. They'll last longer if stored in a clean and dry location, and the wheels might need to be re-inflated occasionally to keep them operating in tip-top shape.

### *Measuring Tape and String*

#### ▷ **Measuring Tape**

Finally, you will need a couple of tools to build your garden beds to give you a neat and organized garden layout that matches your plans. There are plenty of measuring tapes on the market that you can use to measure wood or other materials for beds, calculate the distance between plants or rows of plants, and estimate how far plants will grow over time. It's best to pick a sturdy tape measure that stays straight and flat without being held down. Also, remember to choose a tape measure color and style that you can easily read. Black and yellow are the most contrasting color combinations that allow you to see the numbers on your tape easily.

## ▷ String

You can use almost any kind of string, opting for cost and durability. Garden string can be used with stakes to designate your garden beds' boundaries. This string is very inexpensive, sometimes going for as little as $10 for 800 feet, and you won't have to replace it very often as it's strong enough to be reused countless times.

## CONSIDERING CLIMATE

Now, while raised bed gardening makes it *easier* to garden under challenging climates by protecting your plants from overly wet or poor-quality soil, that doesn't mean that the climate you live in doesn't apply at all. Your local climate has a major role in determining which plants you'll have the easiest time growing and when your planting season begins and ends.

You're familiar with your climate–whether it's usually cold or hot, how much rain falls, when, etc. These traits and more weather-related factors play into whether you should choose seasonal or year-round plants. Choose a variety of plants, and include some that are hardy and can cope with all sorts of weather conditions. For example, if you live in a cloudy area, you don't want to bring home plants that require a ton of direct sunlight to grow to their full potential! If you know of a place you can shop for nursery plants or seeds, the tags or packaging on the plants should give you some idea of how much sun and water each plant needs to thrive.

## PLANT HARDINESS ZONE

The information on the tags and packaging of plants and seeds should also indicate a "plant hardiness zone." These are 13 zones of the United States of America (USA) distinguished by their lowest average winter temperature. The hardiness zone indicated on a plant's tag or a seed packet suggests which of these 13 zones your plant will thrive. Plants won't necessarily die instantly outside of their ideal zone, but if you want your garden to meet its full potential, the zone and the plant species need to match as much as possible!

So how do you find out your zone? The USDA provides a website with an interactive map of the hardiness zones in the USA, which allows you to input your zip code and find out your zone in seconds. This is an excellent tool for new gardeners who aren't sure what kind of plants to look for, but it gets complicated when considering micro-climates or locations where the climate differs from the surrounding area. The average temperature can vary wildly depending on your elevation, how close you are to the ocean, and how sheltered your location is from the wind. If you feel like your area doesn't represent the rest of your zone, there's no shame in asking a more-seasoned gardener for help or doing some research to see if there's any information about gardening in your area.

Finally, don't worry if you're not located in the USA–similar information is available in other countries worldwide! This information is freely available thanks to technology! Gardeners have used USDA guidelines for temperatures worldwide to inform their planting decisions, but official organizations in other countries have also developed zone maps. For example, you can refer to the official Canada Plant Hardiness Zones Map if you're in Canada. In the United Kingdom, you can use the Royal Horticultural Society's Plant Hardiness Zones, etc.

## PLANNING YOUR GARDEN LAYOUT

Learning which plants to sow and knowing which ones grow in what season is integral to a successful garden. For example, broccoli, cauliflower, artichokes, and kale do much better in cold weather, unlike bell peppers or melons. However, don't forget that there's more to the story than just temperature! Even within the same hardiness zone, plants need different amounts of sunlight, water, wind protection, and more to reach their full potential. Plants also can't just get up and move to another part of the garden to be more comfortable. It would be best to decide which plants are going where to ensure they all have what they need to thrive. It can be beneficial to draw out a garden diagram before planting.

A common mistake made by people starting *any* new hobby is taking on too much at once before getting a feel for things. If you're starting your first garden, it's best to start with *one* garden bed for a season to see how it fits into your schedule, lifestyle, and routine. Starting small will allow you to try your hand at raising your favorite vegetables and learn some things from experience before taking on a larger project. More crops will fit into a raised-bed garden than a regular garden, so you'll still get plenty of reward for your work once harvest time rolls around.

### Facing the Elements

#### ▷ Sunlight

When planning your garden layout, the first thing you'll think about will most likely be sunlight. The plant tags or seed packaging at the garden store will include a note such as "full sun" or "partial sun/partial shade" to indicate how much sun a particular plant needs. If a plant needs full sun, it needs to be directly in the sun for at least six hours a day, preferably more. Partial sun or partial shade indicates that shadier conditions work better for the plant. Naturally, you'll want to place "full sun" plants in the sunniest region of your garden, and "partial sun" plants can be placed closer to walls or in the shadow of taller plants and trees. If you have a tall plant that needs direct sun and a short plant that needs shade, you can conveniently plant them next to each other to optimize their growing potential! When planning your garden layout in the spring, be aware that nearby trees and shrubs might grow before the end of the season, creating more shade than you initially bargained. You can use suntraps or shade blankets to artificially create the right sun conditions for your plants in hot or shady regions.

▷ **Water**

Water is just as important as sunlight for plant survival. For convenience, think about where the water source in your garden is located and factor that into where you eventually lay your garden beds. This will cut down how much water you're lugging back and forth each day, but it also makes it easier to give your plants some extra water during a heat-wave without spending too much spare time under the sun.

▷ **Wind**

While some beginner gardeners don't think about this, working wind protection into your garden design is essential. Heavy wind can physically damage your plants and suck moisture from the soil. This is a condition known as "wind-burn." Tall plants like pole-climbing beans, corn, and sunflowers are most susceptible to wind damage and can even be knocked over! Some gardeners plant very close to a wall or fence to guard against the wind, but growing directly next to these can put your plants in danger from the turbulence that forms on the sheltered side. It's a fine idea to use solid fences or walls or just plant a few feet away from the structure itself. You can also use woven fences, hedges, and other non-solid barriers to defend against the wind, as these imperfect shelters break up a gust of wind to make it much less damaging. Additionally, you don't have to worry about turbulence with this barrier.

### Building Structures

Economizing space is essential, therefore, you need to consider your garden beds' shape, size, and layout to get the most out of your harvest. In this section, we'll be using the example of a rectangular wooden raised bed, as these are the most common type, although raised beds can be extrapolated into other shapes. The great thing about raised bed gardening is the potential for creativity and customization. There's no rule against stepping outside the box (no pun intended, or perhaps it was!).

While the typical raised bed is rectangular, it can be any shape, even star-shaped! For example, if you're building wooden frames for the raised beds yourself and see that there's room in the corner of your garden, you can maximize your use by creating an L-shaped bed. While garden beds can be too big, the size of your raised beds can also vary massively depending on multiple reasons:

- The space you have available.
- Your accessibility needs.

- The number of plants you want to grow.

Before you set out to build your raised beds for the garden of your dreams, carefully look at the space you have available to determine how you will layout your beds. While beginners should start with one bed, you may already be thinking about what your garden will look like down the line, or you might be an experienced gardener ready to build more than one. Being able to move around and between your beds is essential when determining the layout of your garden. Easy access will make working in your garden much easier and quicker while protecting your plants from getting trampled. Your garden beds should be laid out to create a wide central path. This path should be at least four feet wide to allow easy access for wheelbarrows and, if necessary, wheelchairs without damaging your plants. Your garden might also need to be accessible by a small truck to bring in equipment and supplies, therefore making it at least 10 feet wide. A wide, accessible central path doesn't just make it easier to move supplies and equipment in and out; it also provides room for you and your family to gather and enjoy the garden you've worked so hard to maintain. Having a wide central path also makes it easier for more than one person to work in the garden simultaneously.

How big should your garden beds be? There are a couple of guidelines, but it's up to you for the most part. The most crucial factor to consider is that you and anyone else working in the garden bed need to reach all aspects comfortably, without strain or too much stretching. A good rule of thumb with a rectangular bed is to make sure that you can reach the center of the bed with room to spare when standing or kneeling on each side. This will, of course, depend on whether or not the bed is free-standing or if it is a frame built on the ground. This factors out to a maximum width of four feet across for most adults, but adjust to two or three feet if your garden needs to be wheelchair accessible.

Being able to reach all parts of your raised bed mostly depends on the width of the bed, and while the length isn't quite as important, there are still a couple of things to consider. Firstly, consider the price of lumber required to build a very large bed–it starts getting much more expensive if you exceed 12 feet. If you're on a tight budget, it's best to keep your bed lengths shorter than that. Secondly, a very long bed that you can't step over can be a nuisance when getting around your garden. You don't want to walk *on* garden beds, as you may potentially damage your plants, and it can mess up the soil and cause it to compact.

There are a couple more things to keep in mind when it comes to the length and width of your garden beds. Lumber comes in 8, 10, and 12-foot lengths, which can be easily divided into two, three, four, and six-foot-long pieces. For example, an 8-foot piece of lumber and a 12-foot piece of lumber can both be sawed in half and used to make a garden bed that is four feet long and six feet wide. Factoring the size of the lumber you're buying into the size of your garden beds will cut down on waste, saving you work and money in the long run. Secondly, don't forget that you need to fill the garden bed with soil, making larger beds much more expensive and a lot more work.

The amount of soil you'll need is also a major factor in deciding how tall or deep your garden beds need to be. To give your plants' roots room to grow, they should have about 10 inches of loose soil at their disposal, at an absolute minimum. If you're planting carrots, squash, potatoes, parsnips, or other plants with extra-deep roots, you should take this up to 12-18 inches. The roots of these plants need at least that much loose soil to absorb nutrients and grow well, and the packed ground beneath the raised bed doesn't count!

You may also need to make your raised bed taller for accessibility reasons. If wheelchair access is required, the recommended height for beds is 24 inches, and if you need to minimize bending over, take it up to 36 inches at a minimum.

There are plenty of reasons to make your raised bed taller than the minimum 10 inches, from plant welfare to accessibility to convenience, but if your raised bed is just a wooden frame on the ground, this will take a lot more soil to fill. If you build a 10-18 inch raised bed with a bottom, you can lift it off the ground using legs, blocks, or a foundation without buying and adding more soil. Just make sure the structure of the container can support the weight of the soil or plants. It would be catastrophic to wake up one morning to find that the bottom of the container had collapsed, dumping a mound of soil and all of your beloved plants onto the ground! It's also important to remember that water needs to be able to drain out of the container, as most plants need well-drained soil to thrive.

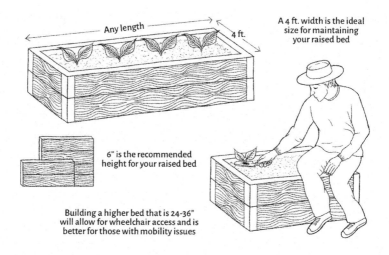

Any length

4 ft.

A 4 ft. width is the ideal size for maintaining your raised bed

6" is the recommended height for your raised bed

Building a higher bed that is 24-36" will allow for wheelchair access and is better for those with mobility issues

# 3

# DAY TWO—BUILDING YOUR GARDEN BEDS

---

*If you have never experienced the joy of accomplishing more than you can imagine, plant a garden.*

— ROBERT BRAULT

---

Now that you have a plan for your first raised bed garden, it's time to start putting that plan into action! Get ready to move out of the planning phase, but contain that excitement; before you jump up and grab the hammer and nails, there are still a couple of decisions you need to make:

1. Do you know how you will be clearing the land for your beds?
2. Do you know what materials you will be using?
3. Do you know how much soil you will need?

In this chapter, we will dig in and get our hands dirty by covering day two, which includes demystifying the famous no-dig method and building our first raised bed! While you can build your garden beds out of many materials, we will be going over the best choices and doing some simple math to calculate the right amount of soil and compost needed for your garden beds!

## WHY THE NO-DIG METHOD?

We've already touched on the idea that raised bed gardening does not require digging. The no-dig method has become very popular amongst avid gardeners as it is a very effective technique. I'm sure you have been curious about what this method entails and how and why it is used.

The no-dig gardening philosophy is the brainchild of expert gardener Charles Dowding, who questioned the need to dig during his years of experience creating and maintaining gardens. Dowding noticed that digging takes weed seeds buried in the ground and mixes them into your fertile soil and compost, causing them to grow, leaving you with even more work. Digging disturbs the soil's structure and integrity, causing it to lose nutrients much faster, meaning that you'll have to feed your plants much more often. Disrupting the natural structure of the soil in this way also interferes with the way it drains excess water, which is essential to the health of your plants. When it comes to raised bed gardening, digging is unnecessary and counter-productive work that only leads to more work later. If you want to be economical with time, money, and effort, leave the shovel in the shed!

Some readers might be feeling a little skeptical. *No digging at all? Not even to remove the lawn and the weeds on the ground before putting the beds down?* To be frank, when you're constructing a bed to fill with fertile imported soil, what already exists on the ground underneath is pretty inconse-quential, and you don't need to mess with it much. However, if any grass or weeds are present, they should be removed before placement of your raised bed. It ensures that these weeds do not start to sprout and spread throughout your bed.

To prepare the land and smother the grass and weeds, news-paper or cardboard will be placed on the ground where you will eventually place your raised bed frame. Don't worry about the ink used for printing; it is made of soy and is rela-tively harmless; it won't contaminate your crops.

This is a superior method because it improves your soil and requires minimum time, effort, and equipment. If the roots of your plants grow long enough, they may even reach this layer and breakthrough, absorbing nutrients from the decomposing organic material underneath the beds!

### How to Lay New Beds Using the No-Dig Method

A few notes before we get into the nitty-gritty of how to build this kind of garden:

- Firstly, you'll need multiple layers of newspaper or cardboard overlapping at least six inches to prevent weeds from creeping through.
- Secondly, make sure that the newspaper isn't the glossy kind, as this won't decompose properly.
- Thirdly, remember that good drainage is essential for the health of your plants. If there's no grass to smother, and the earth you're placing your beds on top of is very compact, you may want to put down a layer of gravel or loosen up the dirt using your garden fork before you lay down your structures.

This section will give you a step-by-step overview of how best to lay down new beds in your garden without digging.

If there's grass, weeds, or other unwanted plant growth on the spot where you're going to lay down your beds, you need to start by mowing this down. Cut down grass and weeds as close to the ground as you can to prevent unwanted plants from growing into your garden bed; it will also create a nice flat surface to build on. Don't clear away the pile of cut plant matter afterward; it will be great for your garden when it decomposes underneath the raised beds.

In the meantime, fill up a bathtub or large plastic bin with water and soak the newspapers (or cardboard) you will be using at the bottom of your garden beds. Overnight soaking is ideal, but if you're in a hurry, aim for a minimum of two hours. Paper, of course, breaks apart very easily when wet, so it will need to be handled carefully. I use a plastic crate to transport my sodden newspapers to keep them all together.

Next, measure out exactly where your garden beds will be, using stakes and twine. As the adage says, measure twice, cut once. Then, measure and mark an extra two feet of space in all directions. If you only cover the area you're going to fill with soil, weeds will be able to grow up through the cracks between the borders of the newspaper and the garden bed frame.

Cover the entire marked area with wet newspaper or cardboard, ensuring there are no gaps where weeds can creep through—overlap separate pieces of the newspaper at least six inches. Keep adding layers of newspaper or cardboard until you've created a three-inch-thick barrier on top of the ground.

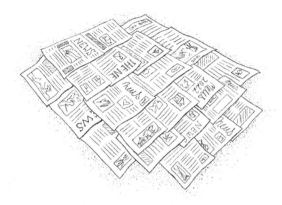

Once your frame is built in the next chapter, you will lay it down on the newspaper layer. Using your spade, fill the raised bed with your growing medium, soil, or a mix of soil and compost. Ensure it extends up to the right height for your intended crops and accessibility needs. Once this is done, there will be an unsightly ring of wet newspaper surrounding the beds, which you can cover with wood chip mulch or gravel to make it more aesthetically pleasing.

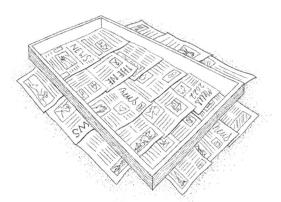

You can start planting as soon as you finish setting up the beds. There's no need to wait for the newspaper layer to decompose. It will have broken down enough that it won't be a barrier to your plants' roots by the time they're long enough to reach it.

When it comes to extremely compact soil, the best solution, without digging, is to grow a cover crop, such as barley or ryegrass, at the end of the planting season. You will not need much soil to sow a cover crop. Once this has grown, mow it down and turn this organic matter into the soil with a fork. These crops will do the hard work of penetrating the soil to loosen it. Covering this area with a good layer of mulch will also help with this process. Bear in mind, however, that this is not a quick fix and will need some time to reap the benefits.

## CHOOSING THE RIGHT MATERIAL TO BUILD YOUR RAISED BEDS

You may be asking, "What material should I use to build my raised bed?" This depends on your budget, style, climate, and overall personal preference. Anything can be used, as long as it has not been treated with chemicals that may potentially leach poisonous materials into your soil. Wood is the most common material used for raised beds and as an organic grower, your choice of timber is integral. These toxic chemicals, which are acceptable for building purposes to prevent the wood from rotting, are unfortunately not the answer for building your raised bed. Specific finishes on the wood can leach into the soil, ultimately contaminating the crops and eventually finding a way into your bloodstream. Again—this is why planning is so important!

There are many types of wood you can choose from, although this will depend on where you live and accessibility. Cedarwood or redwood is amongst the top tier to choose from if you have this freedom of choice. These types of wood are suitable, and an excellent choice as they can ward off termites, not to mention they are aesthetically pleasing. Raised beds built with these types of wood have been known to last ten or more years, making it a worthwhile investment!

Firwood is another reputable and reliable option, as it is on the top end of being hardy against decaying. Hardwoods such as pine, maple, walnut, and cherry, to name a few, will also work well; they are long-lasting and tough.

Consider painting your wood with a non-toxic water-proofing agent to prolong its lifespan with any wood you use. A bonus is that eventually when the wood breaks down, it can be used for organic matter in the garden, so you can't lose out.

### Some Other Options for Raised Beds

Raised beds can be pretty remarkable when considering the vast amounts of unique and creative material options for constructing them. When you are ready to take on and experiment with other versions, here is a list of options you may wish to consider.

### ▷ Rocking Rocks

If you are fortunate enough to have a nearby supply of rocks, you are in the pound seat.

Building a raised bed out of rocks can make quite a magnificent-looking bed. The advantage is that it is more or less permanent or semi-permanent unless you move them, which is not advised. The rocks also add an aesthetic architectural element to your backyard!

The structure of a rocky raised bed (which has a nice ring) can be shaped according to the rocks you have sourced. They can be adapted to fit into the lay of the land. Stack the rocks on top of each other to form the outline of your bed shape. Try to fill as many gaps as possible with smaller rocks to create a 'wall' around the edge.

Keep in mind; that transporting rocks can be expensive as they are heavy. This method can also be quite time-consuming as you need to source the ideal-sized rocks, and moving them around is hard work! If you need to transport them to your property, make sure you have incorporated this into your budget.

▷ **Building Bricks and Cement Blocks**

These materials also work well, as their conformity makes the planning easier. Again, like with rocks, you will have this bed forever. It is also a bit labor-intensive, but it has no maintenance as with rocks. Purchasing and transporting these can also become quite expensive, but the permanence, stability, and next to no upkeep outweigh these factors.

Depending on the type of bricks used, plan your bed while keeping in mind the importance of proper drainage. Some bricks have holes in them, so this counteracts that problem. Using solid bricks that don't have holes, you will need to stack them 'subway style' to create good drainage and airflow gaps.

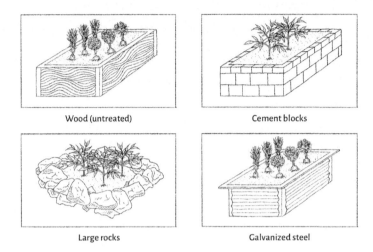

| Wood (untreated) | Cement blocks |

| Large rocks | Galvanized steel |

## ▷ Creative Alternatives

In a world where so much waste is accumulated, consider repurposing items for your raised bed. Besides helping reduce waste and doing your bit to help our planet, some of these items will last long!

Here is a list of some ideas featuring a few options for unique garden beds on a budget. I guarantee that once you start reading this list, you will come up with a bunch of your own ideas.

- Old furniture frames such as beds, tables, or chairs can be adapted to the shape you want for your raised bed and be painted bright colors (non-toxic paint!) to make a bold statement in your garden.

- Bathtubs can make an attractive feature, and they have the drainage part sorted! Although, a few extra holes would be advised.
- Corrugated metal sheeting can work very well. Make sure that the sheets used are the rust-free version.
- Old tires can be repurposed, but some people prefer not to use them due to the chemicals applied during manufacturing. The potential of these leaking into the soil is a risk. You may consider using them for non-edibles if you are uncertain.
- Old plastic kiddie swimming pools for a circular option
- Recycled plastic decking
- Woven alien vegetation to create a 'basket' type of raised bed. Stake out an area and weave freshly cut flexible branches lined with some hessian or other suitable biodegradable fabric. Understandably, this option will only last as long as the vegetation takes to break down.

### Balcony Bed Basics

Perhaps you have a limited area for a garden in your yard, or maybe you have a balcony! Have no fear—you have not been left out of the wonders of raised gardening beds. Therefore, you may try these options out for size.

You may not have enough room to build the suggested wood frame box size, so you may have to scale it down or up to fit into the amount of space you have at your disposal.

Soil is heavy—wet soil is even heavier! Usually, balcony raised beds are built to be waist high and would have a drainage valve system at the base that drains excess water out to flow into a gutter or other outlet. Typically with these raised beds, you will often not be placing them on the ground, so make sure your stakes are long and strong enough to cope with the weight.

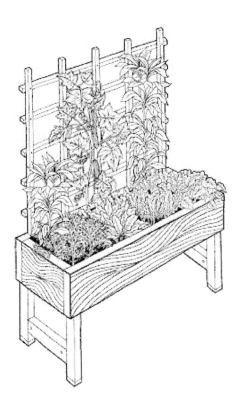

The top tips are:

1. Ensure your bed is deep enough, no less than six inches, so there is adequate space for your roots to 'stretch their feet.'
2. Make sure your balcony is stable enough to carry the weight of plant boxes, although most balconies should be fine. Keep this in mind when the 'box building bug bites' and you want to make many!
3. Attach wheels or rollers to the legs of your box, so it is easy to maneuver.

You may share your knowledge with others who also have limited space for a garden about the benefits of raised beds. That way, you can plant different crops and share your produce! This makes for good neighbor relationship growth too. (Oops, another pun!)

### *Wonderful Wood for Your First Raised Bed*

If you are a beginner building your first raised bed, I recommend beginning with a small-sized wooden frame (4 x 6), as it is a great starting point.

As previously mentioned, wood is the most commonly used natural material for building raised beds. It is sturdy as well as long-lasting. Essentially, you will be building a big box, so, fortunately, if you didn't concentrate in woodworking class, don't despair—you are going to be just fine! You could, of course, choose to go out and buy a ready-made raised bed box, but where is the fun in that? Besides being a bit pricey, your homemade one will give you so much pleasure knowing you made it from scratch, so go on, give it a bang! Yes, you get to use a hammer too.

The tools you will need are:

- Tape measure
- Carpenters pencil
- Drill and a range of drill bits to fit the screws you will be using
- Level
- Hammer or sledgehammer
- Screws
- Spade (for leveling the ground, no digging!)
- Rake
- Saw (this might be necessary if you need to adjust your lengths of wood)

Here are the steps to build a 4 x 6 by 6-inch high raised bed. Head to the lumber store and buy:

- Three 2 x 6 planks measuring 8-feet in length. It doesn't have to be precisely these measurements, but this is what you should aim for.

*Tip: Spare wood will be left over to create the stakes you will need to hold your box together.*

Usually, if they don't have the size you want in stock, the store will be able to cut the wood required to your size specifications. You will often need to purchase the entire piece of wood and take the offcuts home. As an avid gardener, you will find a use for the offcuts. For example, they can be used to make stakes, define paths, make signs, etc.

If the store is not able to cut the wood into the lengths you require, you will need to follow the steps below:

1. Measure and cut two lengths that are four feet in length.
2. Measure and cut two lengths that are six feet in length.
3. Cut the spare wood into 4 pieces measuring 12" long.
4. Layout the planks of wood on the ground, forming a box shape.

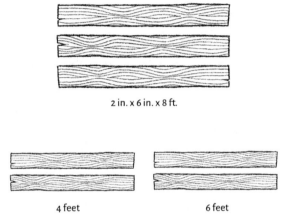

2 in. x 6 in. x 8 ft.

4 feet          6 feet

*Tip: Don't forget to cut your stakes into a v-shape on one side! To keep it neat and tidy, ensure the stakes are all the same length.*

Drill screws into the planks of wood. Make sure the screws are long enough to hold the pieces together securely. I recommend using two-inch screws.

1. Hammer your stakes into each corner of your box.

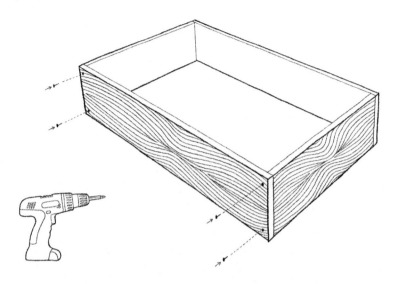

*Tip: I recommend using screws instead of nails as screws have better strength and holding power. Make sure you choose screws suitable for outdoor use, like decking screws.*

1. Make sure your box is level. You can use a spirit level for perfectionists to get it right!
2. You can also hammer in an extra stake on each side of the bed for added stability (point side down). This should not be necessary for this small box, but keep this in mind when you choose to build bigger boxes.

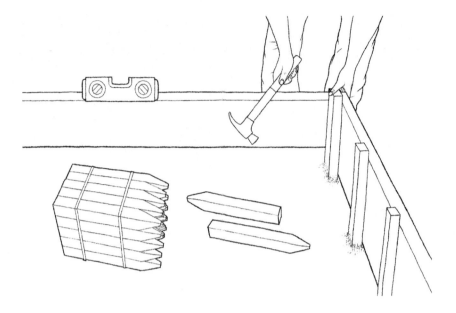

Voila! There you have your first raised bed box!

### *No Frame? No Problem!*

"Hugelkultur," which translates to "hill culture," is a centuries-old method of raised bed gardening that makes creative use of wooden debris like fallen branches to fertilize your garden. Hugelkultur also doesn't require you to build frames or containers for your raised beds. Instead, you'll just be piling up the soil and compost into a mound, or "hill," hence the name.

Hugelkultur is exceptionally cost-effective and sustainable, especially if you live on a property with trees and thus a lot of fallen branches and twigs on the ground. With the hugelkultur method, you'll be putting the resources you already have at hand to use to grow delicious organic food right in your backyard. What could be more sustainable than that?

Building a hugelkultur bed is much like building a regular raised bed, and if you're not a fan of using tools like saws, hammers, and screws, this method will be more straightforward. The first step is to build up a supply of wooden debris. You can start doing this long before you're ready to build the garden. Your wood supply can even include whole logs that have begun to rot due to moisture. Wood chips, fallen branches, twigs, and other small pieces that can be mixed into the soil are also all great choices. The species of tree you're using does matter to a certain extent. Some species will interfere with the growth of your plants. Black walnut is the worst for this, due to the chemicals these trees produce in their wood, and other rot-resistant species like black cherry, black locust, and cedar may do more harm than good. Conifer wood should be allowed to age before getting mixed into your garden. On the other hand, maple, oak, and softwoods like apple, cottonwood, birch, alder, and poplar are safe bets for your hugelkultur beds.

What if you don't have any wood but feel like hugelkultur is the correct method for you? Asking friends, neighbors, and family who live on properties with trees can be a great idea. Additionally, your local power company spends a lot of time clearing wood debris away from electrical equipment. They may have much unwanted wood debris they can drop off, which would go to waste; otherwise, if you're stumped (yes, another pun!) on where to get wooden debris from, give them a call and ask!

After marking out where your beds will be placed, proceed with the method outlined previously by mowing down the grass and weeds in the area and laying down newspaper on top. As with other forms of raised bed gardening, there's no need to dig or till.

Hugelkultur is all about recycling! Instead of adding the frames of traditional raised beds, the next step is to lay down a pile of wood debris. This helps form the "mound" shape these gardens are known for. Next, pile on any other kind of organic debris you have lying around, mixed in with compost and a bit of soil. Make sure the whole mix is at least 12 inches thick on the wood. A vast range of materials can work for this: raked leaves, grass clippings, decomposed manure, straw, and hay are all excellent choices.

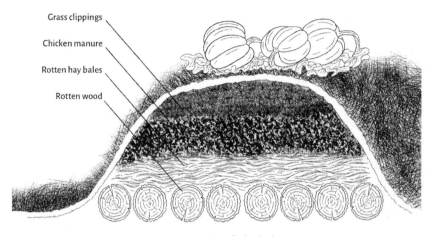

Grass clippings

Chicken manure

Rotten hay bales

Rotten wood

Hugelkultur bed

Let that all sit for a few days before planting to give the pile a chance to settle and start decomposing. In future years, the mounds begin to collapse or develop holes, and weak spots as the wood and other materials break down. You can use more compost to fill in the gaps each spring before you get to work.

**Note:** You can start setting up hugelkultur beds in the fall in preparation for the spring planting season and let them settle over winter if desired. This lets microbes move in and start breaking down the organic materials, adding extra nutrients to the mix before you begin planting. However, you can also build them a few days before planting starts— just remember that new hugelkultur beds are low on nitrogen, an essential nutrient for plant growth. Some plants, like potatoes, don't need as much nitrogen and will be able to thrive in brand new hugelkultur beds, but it's best to reserve plants with high nitrogen needs (like corn, tomatoes, and bell peppers) for older beds that have had more of a chance to decompose.

### No-Dig Drainage: Tips for Healthy Soil

For excellent reasons, we've previously talked about the importance of good drainage. All of your efforts will be for nothing with a poorly drained garden bed, so it's important to take every necessary precaution to ensure that water entering your raised beds also has an easy avenue to drain effectively. If water gets trapped in your garden beds, it will pool wherever gravity allows, potentially drowning your plants. Plant roots won't be able to draw oxygen and nutrients from the soil that is saturated with water, stunting their growth even if it doesn't kill them. Weakened plants like these are prime targets for diseases, pests, and parasites, many of which flourish under wet conditions. Rotting roots are another result of a bed that is saturated. In this section, we've provided a list of ways to improve drainage for your raised bed garden and to help you keep your plants as safe and healthy as possible.

## FILLING THE BEDS

The focus is on creating the absolute best soil you can have for your plants in your raised bed. If your soil is of poor quality, your plants will suffer, and unfortunately, they will not be able to thrive. It is a simple solution: the more organic matter you have in your bed, the better.

An equation of 40% soil, 40% compost, and 20% aeration are ideal. Soil has to have oxygen, or it becomes compact, and water will run off it and not filter through it. If you have too much soil in your raised bed, there is a risk of it all being swept away during heavy rainfall or if it is overwatered.

### Some Soil Math

It is recommended to test your soil pH level before planting, and it is important to test regularly throughout your growing season. This sounds complicated, but it isn't. All it takes is purchasing a soil pH meter that will indicate acidity and alkalinity levels in your soil. You will then have these results to help you buy the correct amounts of lime and other nutrients needed to adjust the levels. Always be careful when adding lime to your soil, as it is easier to raise pH than to lower it.

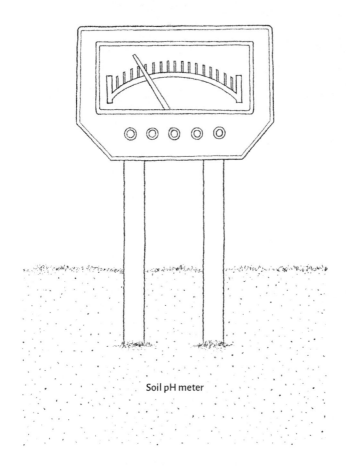

Soil pH meter

Measuring the moisture in your soil is an even more straightforward process. Just stick your finger into the soil about two or three inches deep. If the soil is still dry at this depth, it requires more watering. If it is soggy, then you are overwatering. You can also purchase nitrogen, phosphorus, and potassium (NPK) kits to test whether or not your soil requires more fertilizer. Using all of these options available to you from your closest gardening store will make your life easier and help your garden flourish.

Knowing how much soil you are going to need may seem overwhelming. Don't fret! Here is a guide determining how much soil is required for a 4 x 6 raised bed.

- Convert all of the measurements into the same unit. For example, the bed we are working out soil for is a 4 x 6 by 6-inch high raised bed. You need to multiply the bed's L x W x H in inches:

$$48 \times 72 \times 6 = 20{,}736$$

- To know the cubic feet of soil, you need to divide the answer above by 1,728 (the number of cubic inches in a cubic foot).

$$20{,}736 \text{ divided by } 1{,}728 = 12$$

- If you want to know the cubic yards of soil, you will need to divide the answer above by 46,656 (the number of cubic inches in a cubic yard).

$$20{,}736 \text{ divided by } 46{,}656 = 0.44$$

How much fertilizer to use is roughly calculated by using two to three pounds of fertilizer for every 100 square feet of garden area. Compost layering on top of your raised bed should be at least three inches thick, and the mulch on top of this should be at least the same thickness.

# 4

# DAY THREE—BECOME SEEDS AND SEEDLINGS SAVVY

*Everything that slows us down and forces patience, everything that sets us back into the slow circles of nature, is a help. Gardening is an instrument of grace.*

— MAY SARTON

Now that you've set up your first garden beds and filled them with the best soil you can find, it's time to start planting! This chapter mentions the importance of a garden journal, appropriate care for seeds and or seedlings, watering and how you can take care of your brand new garden before it begins to sprout.

Careful thought about which plants you want to grow is integral to the planning process. Specific selections of vegetables, fruits, and herbs do better in different garden beds with varying conditions and neighbors! The next chapter will follow more about good and bad neighbors in the plant world.

## KNOW YOUR SEASONS AND KEEP A JOURNAL

Figuring out what to plant and when to plant is valuable knowledge. Much will depend on where you are located and the climate conditions. Speak to other successful gardeners in your area and pick up some useful tips from other seasoned gardeners. Most gardeners are usually happy to share knowledge and even share seeds, seedlings, and produce. It is imperative to choose plants you know you will use; planting a raised bed of chilies or green beans is no use if you never eat them. This is about growing food for *your* plate. However, if you find people who want something you can grow but don't personally eat, you can potentially become the established grower of that line of produce for them. The possibilities are endless when it comes to growing food. Many gardeners work with each other and grow different crops, swapping their seeds when harvest time rolls around.

Generally speaking, late fall into early spring is planting time for most plants, but it is not the only time of year to grow. The later in the season you plant will require some more work from you as a gardener to help your plants succeed. Many gardeners swear by planting with moon cycles for a flourishing garden and the best harvests.

You may not know it right now, but you will forget where you planted your tomatoes and what kind of peas you planted... Unless you keep a record!

Keeping a garden journal is an essential component of every gardening journey. It allows you to look back on your progress in your garden to reflect on your successes as well as ways in which you can make adjustments so that you can improve your gardening skills with every passing season!

Record information in your favorite notebook, binder, or app, and keep your journal readily available at your fingertips. Try to journal every other day, and be sure to jot down important information as soon as possible so that it is not forgotten!

Here are some important contents that you may want to record in your journal:

- A sketch of your garden layout
- The date(s) you had sown specific seeds or transplanted seedlings
- What you planted and where
- Germination dates
- Pest problems
- Weather patterns
- A list of plants that fared well and which plants to avoid in the future
- Expenses
- Daily, weekly, and monthly observations
- Pictures of your garden

## BECOME SEEDS AND SEEDLINGS SAVVY

Growing plants from seed add a whole new excitement to growing, as you have involvement immediately! When choosing seeds over seedlings, it also depends on the space you have, as growing your seeds into seedlings does take up a lot of room with all of the trays or containers needed to propagate them. Whichever route you choose, do your utmost when buying seeds or seedlings to find out if they have been organically grown, and ensure that they are also disease-free. Find out if any organic growers in the area are willing to seed swap with you. This is a whole new world that awaits you!

### Sowing Seeds

Choosing seeds for an organic garden comes with responsibility. Many seeds have been genetically modified or have chemicals present. Quality seeds help support diverse agriculture and a healthier planet. So, choose wisely.

Prices of seeds will vary, but the key is to look for these five terms that should be displayed on the seed bags or envelopes:

1. Organic
2. Open-pollinated
3. Heirloom
4. Hybrid
5. Non-GMO

Buying seeds with these terms will be your first step to ensuring and producing a proper organic garden. The next step will be ensuring your soil is rich in nutrients and free from harmful additives.

It is important to remember to stagger the days in which you sow your seeds to prevent waste. For instance, instead of planting your zucchini all at once, you can sow a few seeds every other week for a month. This is known as 'staggered' or 'succession' planting. This technique extends your harvest and prevents too much of the same crop from maturing all at once. As delicious as zucchini is, it would definitely be challenging to consume a large abundance all at once. Pay attention to maturity timelines to avoid planting too late in the season for slower-ripening varieties.

If it is still too cold, consider planting your seeds indoors to start and then transplanting them outside when it has warmed up. If you live in a colder climate, then this is the recommended route to follow when planting your seeds; plus, it gives you a head start for the season!

Ensure to prepare your seed containers well and with care. Planting seeds indoors takes a little planning ahead. You can use trays to plant many seeds or look at biodegradable seed pots that can be easily planted straight into the ground when the time comes to plant them outside. Used egg cartons are perfect for a biodegradable option.

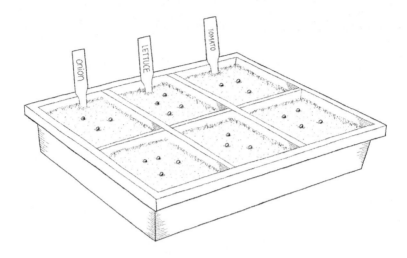

Be sure to use the best quality seed-starting soil. If your soil is of poor quality, you may have to include feeding to improve the soil's nutrients to assist your seeds in sprouting. Don't forget to place trays underneath these containers to catch the excess water. If you have poor lighting and the inclement weather is still casting too much darkness where you have set up your seed nursery, you may need to consider the benefits of setting up a grow light. Seeds will not do well if a gloomy shadow is cast over them! Seeds need at least a day (12 hours) of light to sprout.

You will also need small stakes, such as a wooden popsicle or ice cream sticks, and a permanent marker to label your seeds. (Trust me, you will not remember what you planted and where unless it is labeled!) A light spray of water once the seeds have been planted is sufficient. The aim is to keep the soil moist and damp, not saturated.

The excitement starts while you wait for the first glimpse of growth to pop up and unfurl itself through the soil! This never ceases to amaze me. Nature is just so rewarding.

About a week before your precious seedlings are due to be transplanted, consider putting them into a sheltered place outside to help them acclimatize to their next step. Seedlings cannot handle the shock of moving from a protected environment straight into the elements of living outdoors.

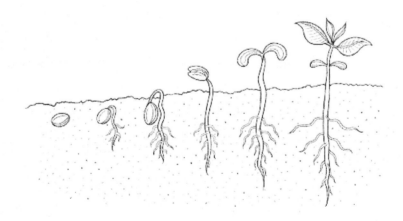

### Transplanting Seedlings

If you have chosen the biodegradable pot method, it is easy peasy as you simply pop them into their designated raised bed. If in plastic containers, carefully pop them out and avoid disturbing the soil surrounding the tender baby roots when planting the seedlings into your raised beds. If you have more than one seedling popping through in one container right next to each other, focus on the bigger and stronger one—don't remove the smaller one just in case you damage the roots of the larger one; nature will sort out the less dominant seedling. Even gently removing it once the stronger one has established itself can work. Gently!

Spacing is critical to achieving a successful harvest. When plants are too close together, there is not enough air circulation for each plant. Planting too closely together causes crowding and can even lead to disease. Another potential outcome is a poor harvest, as the plants are competing for space and nutrients, which may result in plant nutrient deficiencies, limited growth potential, and failure to fruit or flower. Planting too far apart is the lesser of the two evils, but then your yield is minimized. Further along in the next chapter is a chart with the advised spacing of several popular plants.

Seed packets will also give you information about how far apart to plant your seeds, how big the plants will grow (mature size), and whether they need support with trellises.

One of the many benefits of raised beds is that you end up with a higher yield of plants come harvest time because you can plant where you would usually need a pathway to walk for in-ground gardening. Planting in rows or blocks is advised. Don't forget to be mindful of the mature size of your plants, as you will want to place the taller plants at the back of your beds. Think of future shadows over the other plants that may struggle to survive without getting enough sunshine. Don't forget to journal it!

## WATERING WELL

Growing organic doesn't mean that you never water your plants and only rely on rainfall. You will need to water your plants. Water in cities has loads of chemical additives, so a worthy practice in your organic gardening principles is rain-water collection using a rain barrel. Catching your rainwater off your roof and storing it for future use has many benefits for your plants.

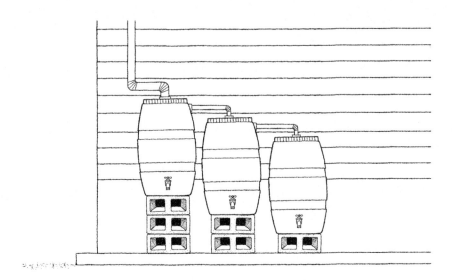

Depending on the area you live in and the level of pollution present, you can also drink the rainwater that you have collected once it has been filtered. To prevent organic litter from accumulating in the barrel, bunch up some chicken wire or fine mesh at the top of the downpipe that would go into the barrel to fill it up, and regularly clean your gutters of leaves and other matter to prevent this build-up.

The rain barrels themselves will need cleaning out periodically, so make sure there is a stop-cock at the bottom of the barrel to allow the sludge build-up to drain out. It's quite fun jumping into an empty barrel to scrub it out! Be sure to time it well between good rainfall.

### *When to Water and When to Not*

When it comes to watering your garden, there are a few guidelines to consider to prevent future problems. If you water too much, you run a high risk of fungal diseases developing on your plants. In the same turn, if you water too little, then your plants will die as the roots will become exposed due to the dry earth. Watering at high pressure with a vast sprinkler circumference is also not a good idea, as much of this water will disappear due to evaporation. Watering at night or early evening will also pose problems, as moisture later in the day that has not had time to dry will encourage pests.

The optimum time to water is in the morning when the sun is not at its strongest, and the ground is cool. This will help your plants have the time to absorb the water and for the foliage to dry off during the day before nightfall.

Watering well fewer times is better than a light sprinkling more often. Be sure that when you are watering your garden, the water is not running off the soil and causing potential erosion, runoff, or flood. Ensure that the water is soaking into the soil where it is needed. Watering at the plant base is what you should be aiming for. You may also be interested in potentially installing a drip irrigation system, as this is far more effective than sprinklers. If you have chosen sprinklers, ensure that they are smaller and have a more direct spray near the base of the plants rather than all over the place.

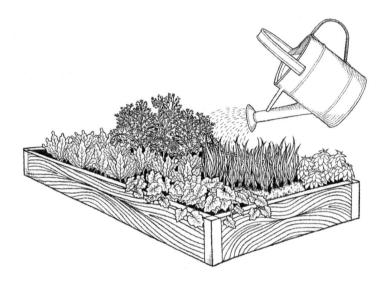

Do the knuckle test to see if your garden needs watering. Stick your finger into the soil. If your second knuckle is still dry when you pull it out, it is watering time for your garden. And, of course, mulching is your friend. So, mulch, mulch, and mulch some more! Mulching helps retain coolness and moisture, reducing the amount of watering you need to do.

# 5

# COMPANION PLANTING

*To forget how to dig the earth and tend the soil is to forget ourselves.*

— MAHATMA GANDHI

K eeping good company is important for both humans and plants. Understanding these relationships between companion planting will lead to a flourishing and wonderful garden.

You may have heard of the "Three Sisters Garden," growing corn, beans, and squash together. These three plants love each other and thrive together. It is such a perfect set-up: The corn grows tall and slender, allowing the beans to shoot their tendrils up and hang on. This duo then leaves enough room for the squash below, which requires a lot of space to spread out in the shaded cool area. The beans also add nitrogen into the soil that both the corn and squash need to thrive.

Companion planting is like this for many other compatible plants such as these three.

Companionship planting is the cornerstone of a fruitful and balanced garden. This method will result in better harvests and even improve the produce flavor. Not only this, but it will also help deter garden pests in an organic and balanced way. Creating this natural diversity in your garden will attract pollinators and benefit the overall health of your soil.

Mankind should take a lesson or two regarding the symbiotic relationship plants have. Understanding how certain crops grow well together has been around for a long time, and it still baffles some scientists as to why.

When growing in raised beds, the space is limited, and the plants are generally closer together, so they must be friends for optimal growth. Thyme makes an excellent team with strawberries as it enhances the flavor, deters pests, and helps smother weeds. Combining other plants, such as creepers or vines, with plants that prefer shady areas can work well, as the creeper provides the shade for the plants that need it.

The plant world is diverse and interesting, full of relationships that need some time to understand. Bear in mind that while there are friends, there are also foes. For example, beans that creep don't like to be planted near chives that can be grown in the shade.

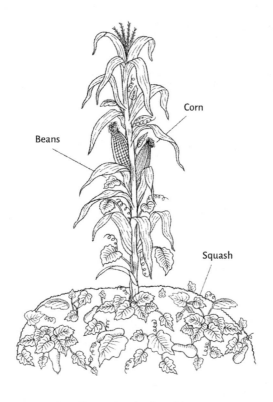

Companion planting with
the Three Sisters method

## KEEPING GOOD COMPANY

Apart from planting your plants as companions for each other, there is also a method that can be used to create a garden that will attract more beneficial insects instead of deterring them. Essentially, the type of gardening we have talked about for your raised beds is polyculture. Although, polyculture takes companion planting a step further and includes planting many kinds of compatible plants in one area that carries a harmonious relationship necessary for the care of each other's growth and development. This way of planting helps minimize the destruction of one particular crop from insects by having other plants in the mix.

The brassica family (broccoli, kale, and cauliflower) attracts aphids, so it is advised to plant these interspersed with good companion plants that deter insects from devouring them. Take plants with high aromas, such as marigolds, dill, leeks, onions, mint, and fennel, and plant them in between your broccoli, kale, and cauliflower to help keep aphids away, as they do not like these intense aromas.

Swiss chard is another plant that sometimes is hassled greatly by aphids, although planting some onions can keep them at bay!

Interestingly, there are also recommendations to plant red and purple vegetables as insects are not attracted to these colors! The notion is that insects are thought not to be able to camouflage themselves on these colorful plants as they can on the green versions where they can hide away from predators—makes a lot of sense! I, for one, am not a fan of red lettuce, but if it is going to help keep the insects away, I happily plant these in my garden.

Marigolds are commonly known amongst laymen gardeners to be natural pest deterrents, but interestingly, when the growing season has finished, you must not remove the plant. Instead, cut them off right at the base, where they pop out of the soil, and leave them with the roots still intact. Marigolds' roots contain a natural and powerful toxic substance that repels harmful root-knot nematodes that affect root plants. So, leave the marigolds there until next season and let them do their magic in the soil. It is also advised that this magic companion plant be planted before planting your veggie seedlings, as they then can create that perfect balance needed to protect your produce! Wow! And they are pretty, too.

## COMPANION PLANTING CHART

A chart has been included for your reference to simplify the wonders of companion planting! This chart has been compiled to feature 25 of the most common plants a beginner gardener would traditionally begin with. Of course, choosing what you want to plant is entirely up to you; however, you may use this as a guideline to jump-start your gardening journey.

Keep in mind this is not a fully inclusive chart. More plants can be added to this list, including more of the 'good friends' and the 'not such good friends' plant species (also known as 'friends' and 'foes') in each row. However, the most common and popular plant selections have been included here.

| Common Name | Scientific Name | Good Friends | Not Such Good Friends! |
|---|---|---|---|
| Basil | Ocimum basilicum | Oregano, peppers, tomatoes | Happy next to any plant! |
| Beans | Phaseolus vulgaris | Cabbage family, carrots, corn, cucumber, peas, potatoes, rosemary, sage, strawberry, tomatoes, thyme | Onion family, chives, leeks, garlic, marigolds, peppers |
| Beetroot | Beta vulgaris | Cabbage family, carrots, corn, cucumber, peas, potatoes, rosemary, sage, strawberry, tomatoes, thyme | Happy next to any plant! |
| Cabbage patch kids: Broccoli Cauliflower Kale | Brassica oleracea | Beans, beets, carrots, chives, cucumber, dill, garlic, lettuce, nasturtium, onion, potatoes, rosemary, sage, spinach, thyme, oregano | Peppers, squash family, strawberry, tomatoes |
| Carrots | Daucos carota | Beans, cabbage family, chives, garlic, leeks, lettuce, onions, parsley, peas, peppers, rosemary | Carrots do not like dill! |
| Cilantro | Coriandrum sativum | Sage, thyme, spinach | Happy next to any plant! |

| Corn | Zea mays | Beans, beets, cucumber, dill, parsley, peas, potatoes, squash family | Celery, tomatoes |
|---|---|---|---|
| Cucumber | Cucumis sativus | Beans, cabbage family, corn, dill, lettuce, nasturtium, peas, onions, peppers, tomatoes | Does not like sage! |
| Dill | Anethum graveolens | Cabbage family, corn, lettuce, cucumber, onion family | Carrots and tomatoes |
| Eggplant | Solanum melongena | Beans, all herbs, tomatoes, peppers, spinach | Happy next to any plant! |
| Garlic Onions Chives Leeks | Allium sativum Allium cepa Allium schoenoprasum Allium porrum | Beets, cabbage family, carrots, dill, lettuce, parsley, sage, swiss chard, strawberries, spinach, tomatoes, thyme | Peas, beans, and sage |
| Lettuce | Lactuca sativa | Beets, cabbage family, carrots, dill, garlic, onion, radishes, sage, spinach, squash family, strawberries, tomatoes, thyme | All plants are happy growing beside it! |
| Marigold | Tagetes | Melon, squash family, tomatoes | Beans |
| Mint | Mentha | Oregano, peas, carrots, cabbage family, tomatoes | Lavender, rosemary, sage, thyme |

| Nasturtium | Tropaeolum | Cabbage family, cucumber, melon, squash family, tomatoes, sage | All plants are happy growing beside it! |
|---|---|---|---|
| Oregano | Origanum spp. | Peppers, eggplant, cabbage family, turnips, brussel sprouts, squash family, beans, cauliflower | All plants are happy growing beside it! |
| Parsnip | Pastinaca sativa | Peas, beans, peppers, tomatoes, lettuce, rosemary, sage | Carrots, celery, dill, fennel |
| Peas | Pisum sativum | Beans, celery, carrots, cucumbers, peppers, tomatoes, spinach, turnips | Onions, garlic, leeks, shallots, chives |
| Potatoes | Solanum tuberosum | Beans, cabbage family, marigolds | Not happy near tomatoes |
| Rosemary | Rosmarinus officinalis | Beans, cabbage family, carrots, peppers, sage, thyme | All plants are happy growing beside it! |
| Sage | Salvia officinalis | Happy near or next to just about any other plant | Cucumber and onion family |
| Spinach | Spinach oleracea | Corn, lettuce, marigold, melon, peas, peppers | All plants are happy growing beside it! |

| | | | |
|---|---|---|---|
| Strawberry | Fragaria x ananassa | Beans, garlic, lettuce, onion, peas, spinach, sage | Not happy to be near the cabbage family |
| Thyme | Thymus vulgaris | Happy to be grown beside everything! | All plants are happy growing beside it! |
| Tomatoes | Solanum lycopersicum | Asparagus, basil, beans, borage, calendula, carrots, chives, lettuce, nasturtium, onion, sage | Cabbage, corn, peppers, potatoes, fennel, walnuts |

## PLANT PROFILES

Taking the plants listed in the companion planting chart and observing the information about each plant in the following chart will help guide you to make the right choices for your raised bed garden. As mentioned previously, this is not an inclusive list, as the possibilities are endless!

Please note: The hardiness zone ratings that have been used in this table are for the United States and Canada, with Zone 1 being the coldest and Zone 13 the hottest, to give you an idea of temperature if you are situated elsewhere in the world.

| Common Name | Family | Growing Season | Hardiness Zone | Best Location (Sun exposure) | Advised Spacing | Germination Period (Seed to harvest) |
|---|---|---|---|---|---|---|
| Basil | Lamiaceae | Summer | 10-11 | Full sun | 4-6 inches | 60 to 90 days |
| Beans | Legumes | Spring | 2-11 | Full sun | 18 inches for bush varieties, 4 inches for pole varieties | 60 days |
| Beetroot | Amaranth | Spring or Fall | 2-11 | Full sun | At least 1 inch | 50 to 60 days |
| *Cabbage patch kids:* Broccoli Cauliflower Kale | Brassica | All year | 1-10 | Full sun | 15 inches | 80 to 180 days |
| Carrots | Apiaceae | Spring or Fall | 8 | Full sun | 1 inch | 70 to 80 days |
| Cilantro | Umbellifers | Late Spring | 5 | Full sun | 2 inches | 45 to 70 days |
| Corn | Grasses | Spring | 3-11 | Full sun | 8 to 12 inches | 70 to 90 days |
| Cucumber | Cucurbits | Summer | 5 | Full sun and sheltered site | 36 to 60 inches | 55 to 65 days |
| Dill | Umbellifers | Spring | 9-11 | Full sun | 2 inches | 90 days |
| Eggplant | Solanaceae | Summer | 4-10 | Full sun | 18 to 13 inches | 100 to 150 days |
| Garlic: Onions Chives Leeks | Amaryllidaceae  Amaryllidaceae | Spring or Fall  Mid-Spring | 1-5  3-10 | Full sun  Full sun or partial shade | 6 inches  6 inches | 90 to 150 days  60 days |
| Lettuce | Daisy | Spring or Fall | 11 | Full sun | 12 to 18 inches | 30 to 70 days |
| Marigold | Daisy | Summer | 7 | Full sun | 1 inch | 60 days |
| Mint | Mints | Spring | 3-8 | Partial Shade | 7 inches | 80 to 100 days |

| Nasturtium | Tropaeolaeae | Summer | 9-11 | Part shade | 12 to 24 inches | 10 to 12 days |
|---|---|---|---|---|---|---|
| Oregano | Mint | Summer | 5-10 | Full sun | 7 to 9 inches | 45 days |
| Parsnip | Umbellifers | Spring | 2-9 | Full sun | 8 to 10 inches | 120 to 180 days |
| Peas | Legumes | Winter to Early Summer | 3-11 | Full sun | 8 to 12 inches | 60 to 70 days |
| Potatoes | Nightshade | Fall | 3-10 | Full sun | 24 to 36 inches | 60 to 90 days |
| Rosemary | Mints | Early Spring | 8-9 | Partial sun | 15 to 20 inches | 80 to 100 days |
| Sage | Mints | Early spring | 4-8 | Medium to full sun | 20 to 25 inches | 120 to 150 days |
| Strawberry | Rose | Mid-Fall | 5-8 | Full sun | 12 to 18 inches | 90 days |
| Thyme | Mints | Spring | 2-10 | Full sun | 20 inches | 14 to 28 days |
| Tomatoes | Nightshade | Late Spring to Early Summer | 5-8 | Full sun | 18 to 24 inches | 90 to 140 days |

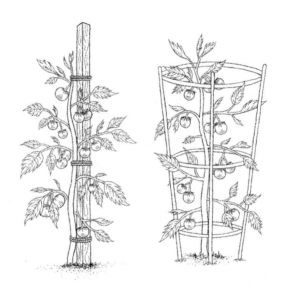

***Basic Example of a Raised Bed Garden Layout***

This is a simplified example, although it will give you a general idea of a typical garden layout. The grayed-out areas are the pathways. Pathways are an important factor to include, as this is how you will be accessing every bed. None of the raised beds in this example back up against any walls or structures.

| Spinach | Swiss chard | Spinach |
|---------|-------------|---------|
|         | Onions      |         |

| Lettuce | Parsley | Cilantro | Lettuce |
|---------|---------|----------|---------|

| Carrots | Beets | Onions |
|---------|-------|--------|

| Peppers | Eggplant | Basil | Oregano |
|---------|----------|-------|---------|

| Marigolds | Cabbage | Broad beans |
|-----------|---------|-------------|
|           | Potatoes |            |

# 6

# GARDENING WITH TENDER LOVING CARE

*I've always felt that having a garden is like having a good and loyal friend.*

— C. Z. GUEST

Treating your raised garden beds as a valued friend will result in you reaping the rewards from your special relationship. If treated right, the raised beds will happily produce healthy plants and gorgeous soil. Raised bed gardening is a relatively low-maintenance type of gardening if you have correctly taken the time to do your planning. Choosing quality soil, mulching regularly, applying fertilizer, and watering wisely are just a few steps to ensure success.

As mentioned in previous chapters, you control the properties of your soil in your raised beds, as opposed to using the soil directly in the ground. Therefore, you aren't stuck constantly trying to amend it. The need to replace all of the soil is scarce and would only happen if you had an infestation of chronic disease in your garden that would warrant this drastic measure.

## HOW TO HARVEST WELL

Some plants are harvested as they start producing, so there is no standard harvesting time to target. Choosing the ideal time to harvest is something that will take some practice. If you leave your crops unharvested for too long, it can potentially lead to disease or be a feast for birds, animals, and bugs.

Bear these points in mind when harvesting:

1. Always be gentle when harvesting, and use two hands to pick. Stems can easily be broken. Unfortunately, this is the end of a plant for the season if this happens. Holding the stem gently but firmly will help prevent it from breaking. You will need to use secateurs to harvest as some plants you will not be able to pick.
2. The absolute best time to harvest your goodies is in the morning. No matter what you are harvesting, this is a golden rule. Your produce will be crisp and fresh in the morning and will undeniably last longer.

If you harvest your produce in the afternoon or the midday heat, it will be limp and will not last as long. If you need to harvest later in the day, for example, you realize that you need a cucumber to complete the salad you are having for dinner, wait until the sun has set and the garden has cooled down before going out to pick your wonderful produce.

### Vegetables

As a general guide, vegetables can be harvested just before they reach their full mature size for ultimate flavor and texture. Allowing them to grow massive may affect the taste as it could be a tasteless vegetable. This is again where your journal will come in handy to record what has worked best and what has not!

Early picking can also stimulate more growth and production. Bigger is not necessarily better in this case! Younger vegetables do taste better! When you notice your garden beginning to produce, make sure to get out there and check your garden every day.

### Herbs

A rule of thumb when it comes to harvesting herbs is to pick the leaves off before any flowers appear, as they will taste better. Snipping off the flowers will stimulate growth and give you more leaves to pick. Basil is a prime example. If you are looking for a lovely big bushy basil plant to harvest, then snip off those flowers as they appear. Dry them out and use them as a natural air freshener!

When harvesting herbs, it is advised to use a pair of sharp scissors and to have clean cuts on your plants only. Clean cuts will stimulate growth; pruning buds with your fingers can cause damage to your plants.

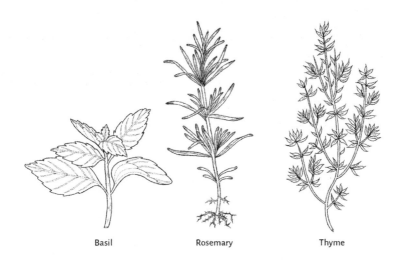

Basil   Rosemary   Thyme

## Fruits

It is possible to grow fruit trees successfully in your raised beds, although even if you are not tackling trees with your first garden, strawberries, tomatoes, and melons are fruits that flourish in raised beds.

When the fruit comes off the plant easily with a gentle tug or twist, it is ready to harvest. Some people get pretty technical with their versions of when a watermelon is ripe from knocking on it or seeing if there is a change of color on the fruit—this will be one of your journeys of discovery. I prefer to pick a bit early and let it ripen on the windowsill, away from potential bugs getting there first!

Don't worry about an overabundant harvest. People will always be happy to take your fresh, organically grown produce off your hands, swap it for something else, or even purchase it! Alternatively, you can also become a whiz at preserves, perhaps...

## PLANT DISEASES

The bane of every gardener's life! Choosing an organic way of growing includes the commitment to not using any poisons. It is possible to have a successful and fruitful garden and not use any pesticides. Selecting disease-resistant plants is worthwhile, especially at the beginning stages. The last thing you want to experience is being completely over-whelmed by disease-ridden plants.

The very first step is to be able to identify disease right from the get-go! Some diseases can wipe out all of your crops, so you need to be vigilant, observant, and aware of the activity within your garden. Inadequate drainage and disrupted airflow, wet weather conditions, insects, heat, and frost are some of the troublemakers when it comes to plant diseases.

One alternative is to cover up your beds, but this can be costly and not practical for everyone. These covers are secured to the frame of the bed that shelters the entire raised bed. They come in the form of hoops, tents, or mini-green-houses that are often retractable, as we still want pollination to occur and do not want to shut out the bees, butterflies, and moths from doing their excellent work.

Crop rotation is an important technique that should be utilized, as this approach simply avoids planting the same crops in the same place year after year. If you plant the same variety repeatedly in the same raised bed, the soil structure will gradually degrade, as the same nutrients are being used from the same source continuously.

Choosing disease-resistant plants and being mindful of how close you are to planting your plants will assist in combating disease. If you are feeling preemptive, go ahead and play detective. Grab yourself a nice big magnifying glass and observe your plants to detect any possible start of disease that may not yet be visible to the naked eye.

Some of the more common diseases and how to deal with them are listed here:

### Rust

This is a fungal disease and is easily identified by rust spots appearing on the leaves of your plants. The affected areas usually start out being an orange color that eventually turns black. Sometimes, even the stems are infected with these spots.

▷ **What to do:**

Use an organic fungicide specifically for rust infestations. Pick off all the infected leaves and burn them. Be sure not to add them to your compost heap or mulch as the rust could spread.

### *Early Blight*

An unsightly fungal disease that appears late in the growing season, early blight will affect the entire plant, causing the leaves to shrivel up and the fruit to become damaged, rotten, and inedible.

▷ **What to do:**

Copper sprays will help get rid of this disease in your plants. Copper sprays are advised once a week, especially after heavy rainfall.

### *Sooty Mold*

This fungus stunts the growth of plants and appears on behalf of certain insects that like to suck on plants to produce a sugary waste secretion known as "honeydew." A charcoal black fungus coating then grows on the honeydew surface of the leaves.

▷ **What to do:**

Dealing with insects is your mission. These include aphids, leafhoppers, and mealybugs. You can get rid of these insects by coating neem oil on the leaves of your plants.

Honeydew will also attract ants, which protect the plant-sucking insects! You have to break the cycle. It is advised to apply a sticky substance around the base of the infected plant, such as Tanglefoot or Vaseline, which can help deter the ant problem.

## Fusarium Wilt

This disease is prevalent during the hot summer months and is triggered by a soil-dwelling fungus called "fusarium." It also goes by the name of "blackened stem." It creates sad, wilted, brown leaves that shrivel up and fall off the plants. It also stunts the growth of the plant and can cause root rot.

▷ **What to do:**

Unfortunately, not much can be done about this nasty one! The advised procedure is to remove the plants entirely and destroy them. The other recommendation is to not plant the same plant species in that place again for five years. I would also remove the soil, dispose of it, and start over, as this fungal disease is difficult to control.

## Mosaic Virus

Although there are many types of mosaic viruses, the tomato mosaic virus will be the one we are focusing on. This disease is prevalent during the hot summer months and is most commonly found on potatoes, peppers, and tomatoes. This disease causes leaves to become mottled and turned into obscure shapes, becoming quite brittle to the touch. Plants may become yellow, and the fruits will be in deformed shapes.

▷ **What to do:**

Once again, there is unfortunately not much to be done to eradicate this disease once it overtakes your plants. Start by removing the entire plant and destroying them. Additionally, it is advised not to plant the same plants in that area again for at least two years, as this virus can live in dry soil for an extended period.

### Black Spot Disease

This fungal disease affects fruits but is commonly found on roses and other flowers. Most often occurring in cool and moist weather conditions, it causes the leaves to drop off after small black spots appear on them. The effects it has on plants will not kill the plants, but it will significantly weaken them, which may cause further issues with diseases in their weakened state.

▷ **What to do:**

A fungicide spray can be used to prevent black spot disease. Check your plants for this during wintertime and remove them if seen. Do not add the leaves you remove to your compost pile; instead, burn them to prevent further spread.

### Powdery Mildew

This disease is easy to spot with its dusty white layer that coats plants' leaves, stems, and flowers. Peas, cucumbers, grapes, apples, and daisies are the plants that are most affected by this nasty mildew.

▷ **What to do:**

Collect the leaves and destroy them to reduce the distribution of spores. Ensure that you are not over-watering or watering at night, and also ensure there is good drainage and air circulation, as these are common causes of this disease.

There are many all-natural fungicides available to apply to your plants, or try out this homemade remedy:

Take one teaspoon of baking soda mixed into one quart (or four cups) of water, put it into a spray bottle, and then spray on the affected area of your plants.

*Downy Mildew*

Downy mildew develops during wet months, presenting as a gray/white colored mold that appears on the underside of the leaves of plants. This mildew will eventually cause these leaves to die. It also has the potential to spread in the soil but will not survive in the winter months. Lettuce, broccoli, and cauliflower are susceptible to this disease.

▷ **What to do:**

Combine one tablespoon of potassium bicarbonate with a gallon (16 cups) of water, and spray liberally all over the affected parts of the plants.

Prevention is always better than having to cure. Water your plants from the bottom; if there is no water on the plant leaves, the mildew cannot spread. Wet leaves are necessary for this type of mildew to invade plants.

You also may try the following:

Combine hydrogen peroxide and baking soda as it creates a powerful anti-fungal solution. It can be used weekly as a preventative measure. It is a two-day process to follow:

**Day one:** Mix six tablespoons of hydrogen peroxide into one gallon of water and spray well all over the infected plants. Be sure to reach all parts of the plants, fruit, leaves, and stems.

**Day two:** Mix two tablespoons of baking soda into one gallon of water and spray liberally again all over your plants.

### *Canker*

Open wounds appear on the leaves that bacterial or fungal pathogens have contaminated. You may also find that the stems and other parts of the plant have become infected. This disease can be severe but not too serious if spotted early.

▷ **What to do:**

Prevent all circumstances of root rot by minding how much you water your plants and how closely the plants are planted together. Remove the diseased parts of the plants and destroy them. Keeping your soil hygienic, healthy, and full of nutrients can help prevent this horrible disease.

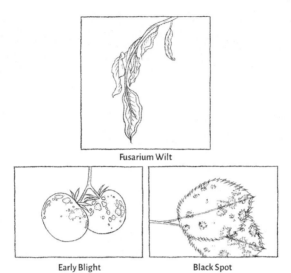

Fusarium Wilt

Early Blight                Black Spot

## FERTILIZERS

There are so many types of fertilizers on the market, but do your homework and make sure the one you are purchasing is, in fact, organic. Many fertilizers contain harmful chemicals! Organic fertilizers work slowly, and this is most beneficial for your soil as the time taken for the soil organisms to break down the fertilizer allows for a slow release of nutrients. This is far more advantageous, as there is no waste, which often happens with the fast release of chemically enhanced fertilizers that have a quick-release effect. The state of your plants will determine the need for fertilizers. If the case is a desperate one, consider liquid fertilizers, as they will work faster than powdered ones.

Fertilizers enhance the soil's natural fertility and work to substitute components taken out of the soil from the previous crops that were planted. When applying fertilizer, there is a process to follow, as it can potentially harm your plants if applied too early. You will need to wait until the plants are developed before fertilizing, as applying it too early can kill them. Young plants cannot handle a massive dose of nutrients, and it will most likely affect their roots if done too early.

A remarkable benefit of balanced and fertilized soil is that the soil ends up being workable and functional as more air is present. This helps the nutrients get to the roots quicker. Apart from this, the bacterial and fungal matter in the soil increases significantly, which is an indicator of healthy soil that will be good for you and your plants.

When your plants mature, a good indication they need fertilizer is when there is discoloration forming, such as yellowing on the leaves. This does not signify early autumn; it simply means, more often than not, that there is a lack of nutrients. Healthy, green, and thriving plants do not need fertilizer, so don't interfere with plants doing well.

You have done an excellent job, and now you can sit back and keep an eye on your plants progress as things change quickly when it comes to gardening and growing your own produce!

Some organic fertilizer options are listed below for you to consider using in your garden.

### Manure

Cow, horse, sheep, and chicken manure are full of organic matter, but it isn't all created equal. Chicken manure tops the list with having the highest nutrient content of all other livestock animal manures. Be cautious when laying manure of any kind near plants, as sometimes it is so rich in organic matter that it has the potential to burn them! Be sure to use manures that have been thoroughly composted for six months or more.

### Shellfish Fertilizer

Smashed-up shells and bones from shellfish constitute shellfish fertilizer, a fantastic source of minerals for your garden, including calcium and phosphorus. This fertilizer contains a compound called "chitin" that is extremely beneficial in combating pest production. This is good stuff to use!

### Fish Emulsion

Fish emulsion fertilizer is used to help speed up plant growth and will help your plants develop stronger roots. It must be diluted with water and used sparsely to prevent any burning of your precious plant roots. It is exceptionally powerful, so be careful not to overuse it and damage your plants.

### Bone Meal

This fertilizer aids in the strengthening of root systems, is excellent for bulb plants and helps grow strong and healthy flowers. Bone meal comes from crushing up animal bones, most often from abattoirs. This fertilizer has a healthy dose of calcium and phosphate. I always pop a handful of bone meal into every hole I plant a tree in.

### Rock Phosphate

Rock phosphate is excellent for establishing roots and bulb plants. It can be either calcium- or lime-based. It looks like crumbly sand that contains high doses of phosphate and other minerals. An interesting fact about rock phosphate is that it does not seep into the soil; it is there purely for the roots of the plants.

### Final Note on Fertilizers

Pay heed to your soil needs before fertilizing. Investing in a soil testing kit is a good investment, as you then will know precisely which compounds you need for your soil and can eliminate any guesswork.

There is a standardized industry labeling system of 'N' for nitrogen, 'P' for phosphorus, and 'K' for potassium and the soil test will use these labels to give you the readings. You may have noticed that fertilizer packaging has these NPK letters displayed. If there are numbers displayed up to 13 for either of these letters individually, then the chances that this fertilizer is not organic are pretty strong. The total number of all three letters should not add up to more than 15 to be organic. Each number is the percentage of what that bag contains. Steer clear of bags that display contents of muriate, urea, nitrate, ammonium, phosphoric, and superphosphate, as these are likely to be chemical-based fertilizers.

The last word on fertilizers is to follow the application instructions to the letter! Applying at the correct time, just before spring, and checking to see if monthly top-ups are needed, is key to a successful, bountiful garden.

## PESKY PEST CONTROL METHODS

Your garden is an ecosystem with a complete needs cycle where every part has to be balanced. If you start putting toxic chemicals into the mix, the balance will be disturbed, and the cycle will be broken. There are always natural alternatives to consider to eradicate pests trashing your garden. An organic garden takes commitment and care to all things living.

Animal-friendly traps can be placed around your garden if you have problems with animals. These harmless traps will capture the rascals, and then you can release them away from your garden. The most important thing about traps is that you must remain consistent in checking on them. The last thing you want to find is a dead animal that has suffered from your forgetfulness!

Birds can be deterred from your garden by placing netting over your fruit or vegetables, either individually, which can be time-consuming, or by stretching a net over a frame that covers the beds.

Cats can be prevented from digging and doing business in your garden with a simple method of placing pinecones beside your plants, as cats do not like the prickly texture.

Another method is to place meshed wire or chicken wire between your plants and at the edge of your beds. Fencing, nets, and covers will offer the best protection depending on your budget, as this option can run up the costs quite quickly!

*Side note: If your beds are 36 inches high or taller, rabbits and some other pests are unable to reach them. Another reason why raised beds are a win!*

### Recommended Organic Pesticides

Keep in mind that these pesticides, even though organic, can potentially be harmful to your plants, the soil, and even yourself if not used carefully. After all, they are created to eliminate pests and insects that create havoc in your garden. Therefore, please proceed with utmost caution when using any of these suggestions.

Using these mixtures for existing bug treatments and preventative measures is advised, either in the morning or early evening. It is not recommended to use these mixtures in the middle of the day when it is very sunny or humid.

If it rains after spraying, you will need to reapply for efficacy as with all sprays.

## ▷ Neem Oil Spray

This is a buzzword among many organic growers as neem oil has tremendous deterrence and effectiveness as a pesticide. Neem oil will disturb the hormonal process of insects that feast on plants. The oil is sourced from neem tree seeds and is a very effective and natural insecticide that targets all the phases of insects' life cycle, including egg, larvae, and adult stages. It is handy for a selection of all garden pests and is also a natural fungicide that is brilliant for getting rid of mildew and other fungal diseases that affect plants. Neem oil is also biodegradable, and even though very effective against pests, it is non-toxic, so it will not affect your domestic animals, birdlife, fish, and other wild animals. It is relatively easy to source in your general plant nursery outlets and food markets.

The general dosage is two teaspoons of neem oil to one quart of water, mixed by shaking well, and then sprayed onto the affected plants. Apart from using it during infestations, it can also be used as a preventative measure in your garden.

▷ **Vegetable Oil Spray**

Vegetable oil spray can be used for infected plants and preventative measures. Using a general oil base such as vegetable oil can be very effective in getting rid of pesky bugs! Combine one tablespoon of vegetable oil, one table-spoon of baking soda, and one gallon of water. This will coat the plant with a slippery mixture that will ultimately asphyx-iate bugs that dare to tread where you have sprayed by blocking their breathing.

▷ **Garlic Spray**

Garlic has a pungent aroma and is known for its natural fungicidal and pesticidal properties. Take two large cloves, pulverize them with a bit of water to make a smooth puree texture, and let it sit overnight. In the morning, mix this with a quart of water and use it as a repellent spray. Use very liberally and soak the entire plant. This can also be used for preventative measures.

## ▷ Chili Pepper Spray

Chili pepper spray irritates the outer shells of soft-body insects like aphids, mealy bugs, caterpillars, and maggots.

When using fresh chilies, blend as you would have done with the fresh garlic, using half a cup of chilies and water. When combined, add another cup of water and put it on the stove to bring to a boil. Once boiled, allow to cool and then strain into a jar.

When using chili powder, mix up one tablespoon of powder with one quart of water. Mix well and spray liberally.

Use this spray for both current infections or as a preventative spray.

You can also use a mixture of garlic and chilies to make a potent spray.

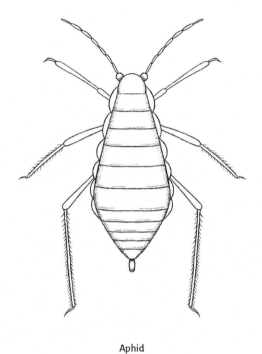

Aphid

## ▷ Tomato Leaf Spray

Tomatoes are amongst the nightshade family of plants and are very effective in combating the effects of aphids and other insects naturally. This is due to an alkaloid they contain called "tomatine." Pick a bunch of leaves from the base of the tomato plant and mix them into a quart of water that is left to steep overnight. In the morning, strain and then spray all over your plants. If you have a lot of tomato plants, this is the most cost-effective insecticide method available. It is said to be very effective.

## ▷ Diatomaceous Earth

Interestingly, diatomaceous earth is known to form about 26% of the earth's crust by weight! This is an entirely natural and abundant material formed from metamorphic rock created by fossilized algae known as diatoms, hence the rather cumbersome word to describe it!

This natural product is effective in suffocating insects in a somewhat abrasive way. It soaks up the waxy substance on the insect's outer 'shell' (or skeleton) and ultimately dries them to death!

It is a powder, and it needs to be reapplied if it rains. A tip is to use a spoon to spread it, as the powder sticks to your hands, and yes, you guessed it, it dries out your skin! Make sure you get the powder right up to the stem of each plant and form a circle around each one.

### Final Note on Organic Pesticides

Many organic and natural pesticides are available, but give it a bash at making your own; it is quite simple, and you will already have most of the ingredients at home.

Whatever you do to combat the onslaught of insects, bear in mind to keep a balance, so you don't destroy your ecosystem.

To retain a healthy balance, you need some insects and must be prepared to sacrifice some loss to your harvest to keep this in place. Ladybugs, stick insects, praying mantises, and others will benefit your garden and help retain the fragile balance.

# 7

# COMMON CHALLENGES

*There are no gardening mistakes, only experiments.*

— JANET KILBURN PHILLIPS

There is no such thing as a perfect garden—it is just not possible. When you are dealing with Mother Nature, there are no guarantees. Which type of beans fares better in the heat? Why didn't my onions sprout? Your green thumb will come due to the mistakes you make along the way.

With that being said, gardening can teach us a lot about life! It may seem that the challenges ahead seem insurmountable, although gardening misadventures are simply experiments, so don't be paralyzed by the feeling of failure. Overcoming obstacles is what makes great gardeners. As long as you are mindful that the glorious blunders of the gardening world are a continuous learning process, you will flourish. So don't throw in the "trowel" at your first sign of a debacle; keep plugging away.

Taking special care when creating a garden that you can manage effectively is your first step. It will not be conducive and will only be disappointing if you start too big initially. Start small, and then expand slowly.

## WHAT TO DO ABOUT THOSE WEEDS

Every garden has weeds, and sometimes even some of these weeds are good for your garden, serving as living mulch. Many weeds are also helpful for medicinal purposes, but they are often unwanted and a nuisance when starting a small garden.

Weeds need to be controlled; otherwise, they may take over the actual plants you are growing. Establishing a good soil mix and having a decent layer of mulch will help keep the weeds at bay, and if they do pop through, they will be easier to remove, as the soil will be aerated. Mulch comes in a few forms; however, organic mulch is preferred. Like the plants we are growing, weeds need sunlight to thrive, so mulch will assist in smothering them. The more organic matter in your raised beds, the fewer weeds you will have. Other mulch options are pebbles and small stones, although, bear in mind, they will add no nutrients to the soil. Grass clippings, straw, bark, wood chips, and even layers of newspaper covered with soil will do the trick.

Don't be tempted to use quick-fix systems to remove weeds, such as strong herbicides, pesticides, and fungicides laced with harmful chemicals. They may kill the weeds, but they will also be harmful to your soil. Pulling out weeds by hand is the most environmentally friendly option but is time-consuming. The weeds you pull out and collect can be left in the sun to dry out and then be added to your compost bin. Don't put fresh weeds into your compost as they may have seeds and could eventually spread, creating many problems.

### Weed Whackers

**Borax:** This is a common cleaning product used in the home and can be used for weeds. In 2.5 gallons of water, add in 10 ounces of borax and mix well. Put the mixture into a spray bottle and take special care to only spray the weeds and not your plants. Be cautious not to saturate the soil, either.

**Salt and vinegar:** No, not for your chips! Mix up a cup of salt to one gallon of vinegar and use this as a spray directly on your weeds. Additionally, you can add in some essential oils like citronella or clove.

**Vinegar:** You can also use vinegar on its own. Try to find vinegar at an industrial strength rather than the shop-bought version. The industrial strength is around 20% acetic acid, and the shop version is about 5%, which is quite a big difference. Spray directly onto the leaves of the weeds, and again be cautious not to spray onto the soil.

**Boiling water:** Pouring boiling water directly onto the weeds is an age-old weed-killing method. It works best on driveways or paved areas where you can control the water spillage to a degree.

**Salt:** Sodium chloride, better known as salt, is very efficient at removing weeds. The risks of contaminating the soil are high, so extreme caution is advised if you choose this method. Make sure you only spray the weeds' leaves directly, not your plants or the soil. Generally, the spray uses a one-part salt to eight parts hot water. Do not go more potent than one to three parts of salt.

**Heat:** Not highly recommended, but something to try if all else fails. The heat from a flame-weeding tool will immediately kill weeds. These can be purchased at gardening centers or outlets. This is risky, as you need to be extremely cautious—you don't want to set your garden on fire or the neighborhood! This method is only to be used as an absolute last resort, and of course, when there is no wind.

Let's recap on the important factors required for your garden to survive and thrive!

### Getting the Location Right

Choosing the right area for your raised beds is critical, whether in an ample open garden space or on your balcony.

Your garden must have at least six hours a day, or your plants will not be happy. This is not something to rush into. Choosing what you want to plant is the first step, and then consider being reasonable about the space and the time you have to commit. If you are limited in choice, take your time planning to ensure the most successful outcome.

### Logistical Layouts

Spending time drawing out your plan is vital. Mapping the area you have to fit the number of raised beds you envision will create the best outcome for your garden. What you may have in mind for your layout might be completely different from what is practical or even possible. Raised beds that are too wide, close together, or far apart could present issues in the future. Mapping your layout with accurate measurements to scale will determine the best-sized beds for your space. Also, consider the area you need to walk in between the beds to work in the garden. This also applies to balcony-raised beds, as it is futile if you build a massive bed on your balcony that you cannot reach across and access properly without climbing into it. This sounds silly, but it has happened to some people who have planned poorly.

### Wise Water Choices

Choosing the correct location boils down to how you will water your garden. You may be using a hose, setting up irrigation, or a good old-fashioned watering can to water your garden. Whatever watering method you will be using, be sure that watering your garden will not be a total drama. Having a convenient water source nearby is essential. Lugging hoses across vast areas is heavy, time-consuming, and can damage your hoses and plants; never mind its toll on your back and arms.

Setting up irrigation is costly and needs to be planned. Moving irrigation is time-consuming and is not very cost-effective either. Drip feed irrigation is your optimum choice if this fits within your budget.

### Risky Material Choices

Your choice should not be taken lightly regarding what materials you will use for your raised bed frames. Choosing treated wood is not wise for reasons we have covered in earlier chapters, but it is worth mentioning again. Picking hard-wearing and rot-resistant wood, such as oak, redwood, teak, or beech, is practical. Please choose the most expensive material you can afford; it will save you a lot in the long run.

### Suitable Soil

Even if you have a perfectly laid out garden with beautifully built raised beds, your garden will suffer if the soil in your raised bed is of poor quality. Making sure your soil is the best possible soil you can create by adding nutrients when needed and mulching often is vital. The soil in raised beds tends to dry out and become problematic if not aerated correctly. Therefore, your raised bed will regularly need tender loving care to keep it in tip-top shape. Raised beds are often so popular because, generally, the existing soil quality for in-ground gardening is poor, so installing a raised bed helps with this challenge as you have less soil to amend. Depending on the soil that you will be adding into your raised bed, sometimes including a layer of rocks at the bottom will help a great deal to keep the soil in place. Adding a layer of rocks will also help aeration and establish good drainage. If you are consistent with your mulching and feeding, you shouldn't have any problems. Remember mulch, mulch, and mulch some more!

### Planting Poorly

Unfortunately, choosing the incorrect plants for your beds, be it too large or even too small, does not give your garden an advantage or leverage to have a successful season. If you can, avoid overcrowding and planting too close together or too far apart. Take the time to educate yourself about companion planting, hardiness zones, and how to protect your plants.

### Composting Correctly

Creating a good compost heap is essential if you have the means. When adding compost into your raised bed, always choose the best quality you can find if you don't have enough of your own compost produced just yet. Keep in mind that tomatoes and pepper plants have many seeds that are not ideal for chucking into the compost heap.

### Keeping the Balance

This chapter is not to discourage you but to highlight some of the challenges you may encounter. The best thing about gardening is the constant learning and discovery. It is a never-ending process, but the results of eating your home-grown food make all of these challenges seem quite insignificant.

# 8

# PREPARING AND PLANNING FOR NEXT SEASON

*The fires burn and the kettles sing, and earth sinks to rest until next spring.*

— ELIZABETH COATSWORTH

The life of a gardener is like a clock: it is continuous and never stops. To tend to a garden takes deep commitment and care. With each growing season behind you, you gain more experience and knowledge, which will benefit your preparations for each coming season.

## PREPPING AND PLANNING FOR NEXT SEASON

Set some time aside in the fall to start your planning and preparations for the next season. Include some time to give your beds a chance to rest and settle. During this time, the compost has an opportunity to break down and revitalize the soil once again before the planting begins in earnest spring. As mentioned in previous chapters, now is the ideal time to do a soil test. Knowing the details and levels of your soil will help you determine what your soil needs. Think of it as a way of your soil speaking to you!

Cleaning out all of the old plants and tilling the soil, if necessary, is part of the process. When the soil is tilled, it is aerated by creating little pockets of air that provide oxygen to the next batch of plants. Roots and stems from the previous crops planted in the raised beds will be broken down, resulting in more organic matter. Getting rid of the weeds and ending up with soil that is so beautifully soft and rich in nutrients that you can sink your fingers into easily is what you are aiming for.

Not all plants need to be removed. You can leave your perennial herbs in place and continue harvesting these throughout the winter. Sage, chives, oregano, rosemary, and thyme are some herbs that will manage through winter if you protect them with a cover from the frost. Cover crops are an excellent idea to plant in your raised beds for winter as they play an effective role by stunting the growth of weeds. These can be buckwheat, rye, oats, and even clover crops. A general rule of thumb is to plant these cover crops approximately a month before that hard frost time! Once again, the seed packets will indicate which plants will fare best for your specific location.

Remove all of the stakes, cages, and covers you have installed for your raised beds during the growing season and pack them away for next spring. All labels and other items to mark what is in your beds should also be packed away. Compiling a list of what you have stored away is helpful for you in planning for the next growing season so you know what you have on hand and what can be reused. Again, that journal is handy!

There is no valid reason for removing soil from your raised beds during this time of rest. Adding a generous dose of compost and finally covering the bed with leaves, grass, straw, or even a tarp or sheet will do. Sometimes, covering the entire bed with newspapers or cardboard covered with a tarp can be left to break down during this stage. Another tip is to add some worms, especially those red wigglers, as they will do tremendous work for you in getting your beds in tip-top shape, ready for your next batch of planting in the spring. You may also add organic matter such as table scraps to your beds throughout the winter.

Before the big freeze sets in, you may also choose to plant some garlic. Plant each clove with the flat side down and pointy side up; otherwise, it will not grow! Place a nice substantial layer of mulch on top of the area where you have planted the garlic, as the plants will go dormant during winter. You will be in for a lovely surprise when it warms up in spring, as they will carry on growing right from when they went dormant.

### Crop Rotation

A little bit about crop rotation was mentioned in one of the previous chapters. It is a worthwhile and important system to incorporate into your plans, particularly if you have several raised beds. You also don't need to wait until the end of the season to do crop rotation; this can be practiced midway during the growing season. For example, lettuce has a relatively quick turnaround for harvesting, so either carrots or cucumbers could be planted in that bed afterward.

Crop rotation will significantly reduce the risk of pests and diseases occurring. Think of it as the plants doing the work for you. Instilling this practice into your gardening will make the most of the nutrients that exist in the soil. Plants will have several different requirements and are vulnerable to various pests that will stunt their growth or even kill them. If the same plants are planted in the same place year after year, these plants continuously absorb the same nutrients from that soil repeatedly. The nasty bugs get used to this quickly, settle in, and spread the word to their bug families that there are easy pickings right here, so come on over, my bug family!

It is called "monoculture" when the same crops are repeatedly planted in the same place. This method increases the need for more and more fertilizers and pesticides that are chemically enhanced to deal with the pest problems that occur from using this method—this method of growing upsets the balance of the ecosystem and is not advised. Sticking to crop rotation mitigates this by naturally putting nutrients back into the soil.

There are four groups for crop rotation: legumes, root vegetables, leafy greens, and fruit-bearing. If you split up your beds into these four groups and rotate them, you will not have the same plants planted in the same beds more than once in that four-year cycle.

### *That Journal Again*

No one can keep track of everything unless you are telepathic or have a photogenic memory, which I am assuming is not the case. So again, I reiterate the importance of noting down what happened during your growing season, where you planted what, and your plan for next season. This will help you to improve year after year.

It is tempting to go out there and plant when the weather is good, but it is also helpful to have some information on past events and a history of weather conditions to keep you on track. Creating a planting calendar is also recommended. Here are a few steps to help you formulate one:

▷ **First step:**

Finding out when the last spring frost occurred in your area will give you a head start in knowing if and when there may be a need to protect your plants. At the same time, mark this date on your calendar, so you know to work backward from then for the cooler season plants that will need to be planted before this date. You would then count forward from this date for the warmer season plants.

▷ **Second step:**

Get all of those seeds sorted out to figure out when they need to be planted, so you have a plan and create your planting list. Some seeds will need to be grown inside first, so list those separately as your indoor planting list. Create an outdoor seed planting list, too. If you chose to buy seedlings, your list would skip this step and feature only the seeds.

Take notes on what seeds you planted, and the time it took for your seeds to sprout to the seedling stage to be ready for transplanting into your raised beds.

▷ **Third step:**

Plan when you will plant your seeds, and the expected time it will take for the seedlings to grow and be ready for transplanting. This will be defined by learning from your past experiences from the last planting season.

It is also important to note the dates these will be planted into the raised beds and where their placement will be for keeping note of your crop rotation system. A record like this will also help keep your crop rotation system on track without making mistakes.

▷ **Fourth step:**

Take notes of the dates in which you harvested particular plants and the success rate of each harvest to maintain a record of the time it took to go from seed (or seedling) to harvest. Record all the losses and any significant problems with pests and diseases.

It is easier to create your own personal planting calendar that is specifically aligned to your garden instead of trying to find that seed packet with the information you need.

This may sound overwhelming, but once you have experienced a growing season, it will become easier as you go along. And, of course, you have this book to refer to! Breathe and take it one step at a time.

# CONCLUSION

To garden and eat out of your own garden is the greatest reward a gardener can experience. Sharing your produce with others is yet another reward that is just a pure delight when you see the value of your efforts being enjoyed by others.

There is definitely something quite profound about being able to grow food to eat that is quite difficult to put into words. It is most certainly something that every single person should experience in their lifetime. The experience can even align itself with something quite spiritual for some.

The tools of this trade that have been shared in this book are to inspire and delight you to take that step to experience this gift that nature offers us.

Taking all of this information offered in the book and putting it into practice with a successful outcome is the ultimate goal within everyone's reach.

There are many reasons why everyone should attempt to grow their own food, but here are a few that resonate with the message portrayed throughout the book:

- It saves you money.
- Gardens are aesthetically pleasing!
- Organic gardening benefits the environment.
- It is an outdoor classroom for your family and friends.
- It keeps you fit, and you get a boost of vitamin D!
- It is a great stress reliever and a good source of exercise.
- It will give you a sense of pride in your achievements.
- It will teach you about dealing with and adapting to change.
- The food you grow tastes so much better than store-bought produce, and it's fresher!
- You're aware of what has gone into the soil and are secure in knowing that no harmful chemicals have been added.
- And, last but not least, it is hard work, but FUN too!

Happy planting (and planning!)

If you enjoyed this book, I would generously like to invite you to leave a review on Amazon. I would be incredibly grateful to receive any feedback from readers!

# REFERENCES

Almanac, O. F. (2021a). *Starting Seeds Indoors: How and When to Start Seeds.* Almanac.com. https://www.almanac.com/content/starting-seeds-indoors

Almanac, O. F. (2021b). *When to Harvest Vegetables and Fruit for Best Flavor.* Www.almanac.com. https://www.almanac.com/when-harvest-vegetables-and-fruit

Almanac, O. F. (2021c). *Where to Put a Vegetable Garden.* Almanac.com. https://www.almanac.com/where-put-vegetable-garden

Angelo. (2019, April 29). *Raised Garden Beds – What Size is Best?* Deep Green Permaculture. https://deepgreenpermaculture.-com/2019/04/29/raised-garden-beds-what-size-is-best/

Ann, C. (2021, February 23). *27 Inspirational Gardening Quotes (With Photos).* The Leafy Little Home. https://leafylittlehome.com/gardening-quotes/

Berle, D., & Westerfield, B. (2020). *Raised Garden Bed Dimensions | UGA Cooperative Extension.* Extension.uga.edu. https://extension.uga.edu/publi-cations/detail.html?number=C1027-4

Besemer, A. T. (2022, April 4). *Transplanting Seedlings Outside: 11 Essential Steps For Success.* Rural Sprout. https://www.ruralsprout.com/transplant-ing-seedlings-outside/

Brault, R. (2019). *The New Robert Brault Reader: Thoughts in a Garden.* The New Robert Brault Reader. http://rbrault.blogspot.com/p/i-sit-in-my-garden-gazing-upon-beauty.html#:~:text=If%20you

Bryant, C. (2022). *7 Reasons to Grow Your Own Organic Vegetable Garden – Chantilly Community Fitness*. Chantillycommunityfitness.com. https://chantillycommunityfitness.com/7-reasons-to-grow-your-own-organic-vegetable-garden/

Carroll, J. (2022). *StackPath*. Www.gardeningknowhow.com. https://www.gardeningknowhow.com/garden-how-to/projects/garden-journal-tips.htm

Cat, D. (2020a). *Homestead and Chill*. Homestead and Chill. https://home-steadandchill.com/

Cat, D. (2020b, March 9). *Companion Planting 101 (w/ Garden Companion Planting Chart)*. Homestead and Chill. https://homesteadandchill.-com/benefits-companion-planting-chart/

Douglas, E. (2018). *How to Kill Grass Under Raised Beds*. Home Guides | SF Gate. https://homeguides.sfgate.com/kill-grass-under-raised-beds-30650.html

Dowding, C. (2020). *Start Out No Dig, one method with cardboard and compost*. Www.youtube.com. https://www.youtube.com/watch?v=0LH6-w57Slw

Dyer, M. H. (2021). *StackPath*. Www.gardeningknowhow.com. https://www.gardeningknowhow.com/garden-how-to/balcony-raised-bed.htm

Easy, E. (2022a). *Companion Planting for Raised Garden Beds*. Eartheasy Guides & Articles. https://learn.eartheasy.com/guides/companion-plant-ing-for-raised-garden-beds/

Easy, E. (2022b). *Control Pests Naturally in Your Raised Garden Beds | Earth-easy Guides & Articles | Eartheasy Guides & Articles*. Learn.eartheasy.com.

https://learn.eartheasy.com/guides/control-pests-naturally-in-your-raised-garden-beds/

Espiritu, K. (2020, October 22). *Raised Bed Covers: Ultimate Plant Protection.* Epic Gardening. https://www.epicgardening.com/raised-bed-covers/

Faires, N. (2017). *10 Excellent Reasons to Use Raised Beds in Your Garden.* Eartheasy Guides & Articles. https://learn.eartheasy.com/articles/10-excellent-reasons-to-use-raised-beds-in-your-garden/

Flanders, D. (2022). *The Proper Way to Water Your Garden.* HGTV. https://www.hgtv.com/outdoors/gardens/planting-and-mainte-nance/the-proper-way-to-water-your-garden

Florida, U. of. (2020). *Raised Beds: Benefits and Maintenance - Gardening Solutions - University of Florida, Institute of Food and Agricultural Sciences.* Gardeningsolutions.ifas.ufl.edu. https://gardeningsolutions.ifas.ufl.e-du/design/types-of-gardens/raised-beds.html

Forrest, S. (2011, August 30). *Pest-fighting Anthocyanins.* PlantwisePlus Blog. https://blog.plantwise.org/2011/08/30/pest-fighting-anthocyanins/

Foundation, Y. I. (2018, March 6). *Companion Planting Chart 1 - PDF Format.* E-Database.org. https://e-database.org/companion-planting-chart-1

Gardena. (2022). *Creating a raised bed on the balcony.* Gardena. https://www.gardena.com/int/garden-life/garden-magazine/creating-a-raised-bed-on-the-balcony-here-is-how/

Gardener, E. (2021a). *Common Raised Bed Mistakes and How to Solve Them.* ECOgardener. https://ecogardener.com/blogs/news/raised-bed-mistakes

Gardener, E. (2021b, August 17). *Choosing the Best Materials for Your Raised*

*Garden Beds*. ECOgardener. https://ecogardener.com/blogs/news/choosing-best-materials-raised-garden-beds

Hagen, L. (2019). *12 gardening tools to buy - essentials for beginners - garden design*. GardenDesign.com. https://www.gardendesign.com/how-to/tools.html

Holt, J. (2017, December 5). *Benefits of Growing and Eating Organic Food*. Organic Growers School. https://organicgrowersschool.org/benefits-of-growing-and-eating-organic-food/

https://www.facebook.com/PlanetNatural. (2018, May 15). *Types of Organic Fertilizers | Planet Natural*. Planet Natural. https://www.planetnatural.com/big-stink/

Iannotti, M. (2019). *Garden Strawberry Plant Profile: Care and Growing Guide*. The Spruce. https://www.thespruce.com/strawberries-1402288

Iannotti, M. (2020). *Tips for Harvesting Vegetables From Your Garden*. The Spruce. https://www.thespruce.com/when-to-harvest-vegetables-1403402

Iannotti, M. (2021a). *How to Grow Sweet, Delicious Carrots*. The Spruce. https://www.thespruce.com/how-to-grow-carrots-in-the-vegetable-garden-1403472

Iannotti, M. (2021b). *Why Raised Bed Gardens Are a Good Way to Go*. The Spruce. https://www.thespruce.com/raised-bed-gardening-1402334

Iannotti, M. (2022a). *Plants A to Z*. The Spruce. https://www.thespruce.com/plants-a-to-z-5116344

Iannotti, M. (2022b). *Start Seeds Indoors for Head Start on the Gardening*

*Season.* The Spruce. https://www.thespruce.com/successful-start-seed-indoors-1402478

Laffler, J. (2015, October 5). *A #CompanionPlanting Chart is a gardener's best friend. Here's why:* Windowbox.com Blog. https://www.windowbox.com/blog/2015/10/05/companion-planting/

Markham, D. (2021, April 6). *8 Natural & Homemade Insecticides: Save Your Garden Without Killing the Earth.* Treehugger. https://www.treehugger.com/natural-homemade-insecticides-save-your-garden-without-killing-earth-4858819

n/a, R. (2020). *How Much Soil Is Needed For A Raised Bed? – GrowerExperts.com.* Growerexperts.com. https://www.growerexperts.com/how-much-garden-soil-for-raised-bed/

Odle, T. (2022). *Know Your Climate Zones Before Plant Shopping | Plant Addicts.* Plantaddicts.com. https://plantaddicts.com/know-your-climate-zones-before-plant-shopping/

Old Farmer's Almanac. (2019a, September 5). *How to Build a Raised Garden Bed.* Old Farmer's Almanac. https://www.almanac.com/content/how-build-raised-garden-bed

Old Farmer's Almanac. (2019b, September 5). *How to Build a Raised Garden Bed.* Old Farmer's Almanac. https://www.almanac.com/content/how-build-raised-garden-bed

Pierce, R. (2020, May 28). *8 Important Tips to Improve Drainage in Your Raised Beds.* MorningChores. https://morningchores.com/raised-beds-drainage/

Randaci, A. (2021, March 10). *Common Plant Diseases & Disease Control for*

*Organic Gardens.* Earth's Ally. https://earthsally.com/disease-control/common-plant-diseases.html

Research Centre, P. N. (2022). *Vegetable Garden Plant Disease Problems.* Planet Natural. https://www.planetnatural.com/vegetable-gardening-guru/plant-diseases/

Roach, M. (2013, April 22). *hugelkultur, nature's raised garden beds.* A Way to Garden. https://awaytogarden.com/hugelkultur-raised-garden-beds/

Rodale Institute. (2018). *Crop Rotations - Rodale Institute.* Rodale Institute. https://rodaleinstitute.org/why-organic/organic-farming-practices/crop-rotations/

Saleem, M. I. (2022). *BUILDING RAISED GARDEN BEDS WITH RECYCLED MATERIALS.* Bed Gardening. https://www.bedgardening.com/building-raised-garden-beds-with-recycled-materials/

Seitz, S. (2021, November 24). *6 Best Seed Catalogs for Organic, Heirloom, Non-GMO Vegetables.* Clean Green Simple. https://cleangreensimple.com/article/best-seed-catalogs/

Src="https://Secure.gravatar.com/Avatar/?s=32, img C., d=mm, May 28, r=g">Luke M., & 2020. (2022). *10 Common Plant Diseases (and How to Treat Them).* Family Handyman. https://www.familyhandyman.com/list/most-common-plant-diseases/

T, C. (2022, February 23). *The 11 Best Mint Companion Plants [& What NOT to Plant Nearby] - Seeds & Grain.* Seedsandgrain.com. https://seedsandgrain.com/mint-companion-plants/

Traficante, B. (2017, April 4). *How Raised Garden Bed Plant Spacing Works Best - Easy Growing Episode #11.* Garden in Minutes®. https://gardeninminutes.com/raised-garden-bed-plant-spacing/

Wright, I., & Reynolds, J. (2019). *I've Always Wondered: is rain better than tap water for plants?* The Conversation. https://theconversation.com/ive-always-wondered-is-rain-better-than-tap-water-for-plants-109714

Yards, N. (2018). *Project Name.* Support.naturalyards.com. https://support-.naturalyards.com/prepare-ground-below-raised-beds/

Printed in Great Britain
by Amazon

38302950R00086